CW01653955

MY SON MY DAUGHTER MY SELF

Personal stories connected by one family and two gay children

Edited by Martin McCormick

My Son, My Daughter, Myself

Self Publishing

Net proceeds from book sales will be donated to Dundalk Outcomers.

For more information, visit our website at
www.myson-mydaughter-myself.org

ISBN 978-0-9923652-0-2
ISBN 978-0-9923652-1-9 (ebook)

This book is dedicated to the possibility that one day everyone in the world can live free and equal.

CONTENTS

INTRODUCTION

Having been raised in a conservative Catholic family in rural Ireland, it caused quite a stir when I came out to my parents in 1995.

It was especially difficult for my mam and dad, as my younger sister came out at the same time, resulting in two out of three children acknowledging they were gay. Both parents struggled to come to terms with the news and didn't know where to turn.

My dad's reaction was to reach out for more information and seek answers to his many questions. Over time he contacted Dundalk Outcomers[1], PFLAG[2] in Dublin, and placed anonymous ads in the local newspapers inviting other parents of gay children to meet up in private.

Some parents responded, and he asked them and other parents he knew if they would be interested in forming a support group. He also started to write a book and asked everyone in our family to write their story, which he intended to share with the group members.

After a poor response for a support group and his request for stories, the project fizzled out, and sadly he passed away in 2003. Worse still, my younger sister passed away in 2008 after a long battle with cancer.

A few years after my dad's death, I found a file at home that contained all the research he had gathered, including his title and framework for the book. The file

1 Social and befriending support group for LGBT community in Dundalk
2 Support group for Parents and Friends of Lesbians and Gays

also contained his story, a poem by my sister, and a letter from a family friend.

Following years of procrastination, I eventually took on completing his project and invited family, relatives and friends to write stories. The response was amazing, and everyone who agreed has contributed freely and authentically.

Though things have changed dramatically in Ireland since we came out, there are still lots of individuals and families around the world struggling with the same issue today. I hope this book of personal stories will be of benefit to them and the challenges they face, which is what my dad intended.

ACKNOWLEDGEMENTS

We are emotional human beings. It's difficult to acknowledge our feelings to ourselves sometimes, let alone anyone else. Therefore I have huge admiration and respect for everyone who has contributed to this book - for sharing their stories so openly and honesty and fully expressing themselves. Their sharing of their humanity will help others do the same.

This book was finally realised as a result of my participation in The Curriculum for Living at Landmark Education. My sincere thanks to all the course leaders, my coach, my group and all the participants. It has been a great experience.

Special mention goes to Austin Butler for his time and creativity in designing the book cover, and to Brendan Lloyd for his patience and attention to detail in the typesetting. Thanks also to Daniela Crawley, Angelo Pantalone and Lynette Walker for proofreading the book.

Finally I'd like to thank my family and friends for their love and support at all times. To my sister Edel, thank you for having the courage to be your true self and in many ways for leading the way. And especially to my dad Peter - thank you for standing by your son and daughter, as well as reaching out to help other families in similar situations.

LOVE

by Peter McCormick

One in 10, a cruel statistic and unavoidable.

Everybody likes to be different. Different dress, different colours, different personalities, distinct traits, different voices, different disablements, different handicaps. But gay different? No thanks, definitely no! no! no! no!

One in 10, they say, are gay different. Gay by birth, not by choice, not by recognisable distinctiveness, but only by a personal creeping awareness that one is not fitting into the mould of the majority. Growing up in secret, unable to flourish and blossom, a stunted maturity for most, driven and restricted by the fear of rejection, and public condemnation. What a life! It's unfair.

Our choice as parents of gay children is that there is no choice. Our parenting role was never intended to be like this. Our dreams, our hopes, all our aspirations had foundations in a romantic future of home, family life, children, grandchildren and a contented lifestyle to old age; all very normal.

This dream lasted until the gay culture came knocking

at our door. For 20 years of marriage we had lived this dream, not knowing that our children were struggling alone with a dark secret.

It became our reality one night in 1995 when our eldest daughter let us know that our only son had told her he was gay. A visit to my son's Dublin accommodation followed, and after a shared drink and chat in his favourite pub, I took my son home that night to share the news with the family.

During the tears and the hugs and the explaining and the listening, the disclosure that our youngest daughter had similar gay feelings was announced by our eldest girl. This was a double blow that really knocked us back.

That night changed our family life forever. Self-doubt and bewilderment replaced our contentment, and blame was privately bounced around in the search for an explanation of the origins for this "abnormality".

We felt completely at a loss at what to do, where to start, which way to go, or who to contact. Each route seemed to be a dead end, and we were restricted by the fact that we could not betray our children's confidence until they themselves had come to terms with their situation.

It was limbo land without openings. Surrounded by darkness, with logic battling with confused thinking of pride of place. Thoughts of gay meaning homosexual, man to man, woman to woman, forbidden by law, dead-ended by the Church, born as rejects of society yet created by the hand of God within a loving relationship. How can this be? How can He allow this to happen?

Where does this fit into the great masterplan? Is it a God mistake? Such were our thoughts.

AIDS, drugs, suicide, alienation, gender changes, marches, protests, friends, families, same-sex marriages, in-laws, strange people, weird persons, symbols, customs, cultures, colours, dress, hairstyles, roughness, coarseness, sex language, greetings, gestures, affection, public expressions, cross-dressers, dykes, butch, drags, bisexual, etc, are some, only some, of the myriad thoughts that persecute the mind during this initiation into homosexuality.

We are a late middle-aged couple set in our ways being forced to restructure our life expectations and thinking, "Why this? Why now? Why you? Why me? Why? Why? Why?" And the answer reaches beyond our knowledge for the present.

A mistake by God, maybe. There is no such thing. All God's creatures, us included, have been created with a role and purpose in mind. We are not mistakes!

As parents of gay children, co-creators in this masterplan, we are part of that plan, and we have been entrusted by their birth to us, to co-operate with God in bringing our offspring to a maturity and completeness in His **LOVE.**

CHERISH

by Anne McCormick

I'll start by saying that hindsight is a wonderful thing. If I had known then what was ahead of me, my feelings would have been so different.

When I discovered that two of my three children were gay, to say I was devastated is putting it mildly. My secure little cocoon fell apart. I was no longer heading in the direction that I had anticipated.

I was 50 years old and had arrived, as I thought, at a great stage in life - family reared and looking forward to spending more time with my husband and ultimately grandchildren. But this was not to be - at least for two of our children.

Seventeen years on it's hard to recall how badly I felt and why, but one can only deal with where we're at, at the time.

Some years later my lovely husband was taken from us after a short illness of five months' duration - at the age of just 60. I was 58. We could have had at least another 20 years together. He was the rock of our family on whom we all relied, but the worst was yet to come.

Edel was diagnosed one year later with breast cancer at just 27. She fought like a tiger to live, but sadly lost her battle just over three years later, aged 30.

To all parents of gay children, I would say **CHERISH** them while you can. We cannot know what is around the corner.

I had difficult times with Edel and couldn't relate to the butch image she was portraying, being very feminine myself, but we both mellowed throughout the years. My son Martin was different. He didn't seem to want to shout it from the rooftop, which was easier for me as I realise parents live in closets, too.

I still have some friends I haven't told and probably won't ever now - I don't feel the need - but I suppose they know anyway.

My big problem was fear - fear of my children being attacked by an intolerant society, and this fear remains for my son.

Most people seem to think that homosexuality is a choice. My god, who would choose it? But if there were more gay people in the world, it would be a much better place.

CREATE

by Martin McCormick

I looked at the note and I just knew that the time had come.

It's difficult to explain, but from that instant I stopped running scared. Any sense of fear dissolved into thin air.

I dreaded this day. In fact, for years I never thought it would come. I had resigned myself to the fact that I would never acknowledge my true feelings and that I would just get on with life as best I could.

Everybody had a cross to bear and this was mine, even though I didn't fully accept it. Most of all I didn't want to disappoint my parents, especially when I discovered there was not only one, but two of us in the family. I knew they would be devastated.

The note my flatmate left beside the telephone explained that my dad was coming to Dublin to deliver a parcel and he wanted to go for a drink afterwards. It was like an inner voice told me his intentions, and I realised without hesitation that I couldn't deny my sexuality any longer. I felt a sense of relief, even though this was only the beginning of a long, arduous path. But it had to be done.

Having delivered the parcel, as if rehearsed my father suggested we go for a drink nearby in Maddigan's in Donnybrook. It was quite amusing to see the frustration on his face when I declined his offer and threw his plan into jeopardy. I wasn't trying to avoid the inevitable; I just had a better suggestion, which was the newly opened Barge Pub down the road.

It was there on a dull evening in February 1995 that I finally confirmed his worst suspicion.

As if on autopilot, we trundled off in the car to Dundalk to face my mother. I remember numbly gazing out of the windscreen, looking at all the things I had said and done, or, to be more precise, all the things that I didn't say and didn't do that had given rise to this situation.

For as far back as I can remember I knew I was gay, even long before I knew what the word meant. It's not just something that I thought or felt - I just was, am and always will be. Whereas I have control over my thoughts and feelings, this is something that is in every fibre of my body. Just like the fact that I have hazel eyes or sallow skin.

It's easy for me to make sense of all this now; however, that wasn't always the case. Like the majority of Irish people, I had a fairly traditional Catholic upbringing. I went to a Catholic primary and secondary school, made my first Holy Communion and Confirmation, and went to mass every Sunday.

My parents were an excellent example to me, provided for my every need, and did the best they could. Many Catholic values that I was taught, I still firmly believe today - perhaps best summarised simply as "love thy neighbour as thyself". However, for whatever reason, the Church's teaching emphasised sin and instilled fear in an effort to steer people in the right direction.

Of course what is "right" and "wrong" in the Bible is open to interpretation. In my case, from an early age I believed that to be gay was an "abomination", or to quote a recent Papal encyclical, "intrinsically evil". Hardly what you would call soft words. In fact, I am sure that this ignorant interpretation of the Bible has been responsible for hundreds of thousands of miserable lives and indeed deaths.

Society at large indirectly ridiculed me, sneered at me, condemned me, even hated me to the point that it had beaten me, the real me, into repression. It would take a strong soul to stand in the face of such prejudice and openly declare, "I am gay and I am proud of who I am". I certainly wasn't capable of that at that stage in my life.

When I caught sight of my mother waiting up in her dressing gown that night, and as she opened her arms to accept me, my sluice gate burst open and an avalanche of bottled-up emotion flooded the world around us. We clung to each other, our hearts wrenched, and we sobbed to the core.

It is without question the most emotional moment of my life. For each of us, though, "coming out" had different implications. For me, it was the dawn of a new era. Though fully aware that a rough ride lay ahead, I was relieved that for the first time in my life I was truly honest with myself.

For my mother and my father, that night spelt disaster - a mixture of despair, blame, guilt, fear, and of course sin.

A visit to Icebreakers, a coming-out group in Dublin, followed shortly afterwards, as did my first relationship with a great guy, which only lasted 10 weeks but resulted in lots of new friends.

It took almost another year to tell my best friend, who, surprisingly, didn't suspect a thing. Realising there was nothing of which to be scared, I gradually told all of my friends and was comforted by the fact that they all stood by me. I have had no adverse reactions, none that are worth worrying about anyway, which proves to me that if you are content with who you are, nobody else's opinion matters.

I sometimes look back to those days, almost six years ago now, and wonder about all the fuss. The wall, which seemed insurmountable then, looks like a stepping stone now. Yes, it's been a roller-coaster ride, full of highs and lows, swings and roundabouts, but the main thing is that I'm on the ride and getting value for money. If only I knew breaking the silence wasn't anywhere near as bad as I had imagined, I would have made the move long ago.

However, I have no regrets. I believe everything happens for a reason, and this was no different. Had I come out earlier, I may not have focused on my career or travelled around the world or met some fantastic people and formed great friendships.

10 YEARS LATER

I wrote that story in response to a request from my dad. He said he wanted to establish a support group in Dundalk for parents of gay children and he wanted to write a book. His idea was to get each of us in the family to write about our experiences, and our stories would be compiled in a book and made available to other families and friends in similar situations.

I thought it was a good idea and eventually put pen to paper, and that is what I wrote. I had intended to write more, but never did, and as a result I never sent my story to him.

At that time I was living in Sydney. On the surface, I had a great life. I was living in a trendy apartment on Bondi Beach, drove a nice car, had a decent job, and was physically in good shape. However, I had got caught up in the Sydney gay scene and was getting wasted most Friday and Saturday nights. My working week would be spent recovering until I was recharged again for the weekend. It was a vicious cycle, and something I knew I had to break.

When my visa came up for renewal, I knew the best thing for me to do was to return home to live in Ireland. It would prove to be a wise and necessary move on many levels.

Within a few months of returning home, my Uncle Gerry died of bowel cancer. Then weeks later, my dad was diagnosed with a brain tumor. The prognosis from the outset wasn't good. Though he was determined to fight and had a positive outlook, the disease would prove to get the better of him. He died five months later, ironically on Edel's birthday. Seven months after that, my Aunty Anne, who was also my godmother, died after a long battle with cancer. Three siblings, killed by cancer, all aged 60. It was a bleak time for all our families.

I didn't cope with my feelings very well. Just like burying my feelings around being gay, I didn't grieve for my dad in the way I should. I returned to work very quickly and put the head down and got on with life.

Not being able to express my feelings was something of which I was very conscious and it concerned me. Since my previous relationship, I hadn't allowed myself to get close to anyone. I was aware that my own behaviour was quite destructive at times and that I should see a counselor.

A good friend of mine had been seeing a psychotherapist, and I had seen a huge change in her during the course of her sessions. So I was inspired to take some action and made an appointment with the same practice, which specialised in group therapy. I initially had a couple of one-on-one sessions, and then I joined a group with considerable trepidation.

This was a whole new experience for me - a forum where people freely shared very personal issues in their lives. Initially I was very reluctant to let go, but bit by bit I began to open up and depend on the group. In fact, it became part of my weekly routine, and much to my surprise I continued to attend for more than three years. I explored a lot over that time, which helped me get in touch with my feelings at a time when I needed an outlet for my emotions. It uncovered feelings of resentment that I didn't realise I had built up towards my mother and best friend, who I felt didn't support me enough after I came out. It took a long time, but eventually I could see my part in what I had created, and I cleared it up with each of them.

A year after dad passed away, much to our horror, Edel was diagnosed with breast cancer. Again, from day one the prognosis wasn't good. The cancer had already spread to her lymph nodes, which meant it was in her bloodstream, and from there it could go anywhere.

However, despite the doctor's opinion, Edel swung into battle and was determined to beat the disease. Within days, she had a mastectomy and was receiving radiotherapy and chemotherapy. She appeared to be making progress as time went by.

However, just as it seemed she was getting somewhere, she would have a major setback, and would be starting from scratch again. Each time Edel was knocked back, she would dust herself down and off she'd go again.

About two years into her illness, her friend Kevin, who was qualified in complementary medicine, believed he could help her. He offered to give up his job and take care of her. In what was a miserable situation, he was a breath of fresh air, offering Edel and our family some hope.

He introduced her to a healthy diet, complementary therapies and The Oasis of Hope - a clinic in Mexico with a holistic approach to cancer treatment. Though the prospect of travelling to Mexico for treatment scared Edel and our family, there was a sense of taking control of events and not just letting them happen.

At €35,000 a trip, the cost was another worry. However, once Edel and Kevin committed to going, everyone got into action to raise money to help fund the trips.

The response was staggering. Friends held concerts, coffee mornings and sports days all across the county. Interviews with the local radio and newspapers helped spread the news, and Edel's willingness to openly share about her illness resonated with a lot of people. A fundraising dinner at a local hotel was attended by more than 540 people. Her bravery in the face of such adversity touched, moved and inspired a whole community.

After three and a half years of fighting cancer, including the best conventional and complementary therapies, two mastectomies, one hip replacement, and two trips to Mexico, Edel could take no more and was taken from us. My little sister who I loved dearly, her life cut so short by a cruel disease. It was heartbreaking. And still is.

I didn't do much in the months that followed. Unlike after my father's death, I didn't rush back into work. Not that there was much choice. The global financial crisis had hit Ireland hard, and jobs were being lost left, right and centre. As did a lot of my former colleagues, I signed on the dole and picked up work where I could.

Saddled with hefty mortgages from acquiring my own home and an investment property in the boom, it was a struggle trying to meet the monthly repayments and survive each month. Then one day out of the blue, I got a call from an old client of mine in Australia, offering me a job in Melbourne. It was an opportunity that I couldn't turn down, and though it was difficult leaving my family and hometown, I returned to Australia to live.

The past couple of years have been pretty good. Thankfully everyone in my life has been in reasonably good health. I'm enjoying my work and I have made some great friends here in Melbourne.

With less worries and having a bit more head space, I was on the lookout for a challenge. Then late last year, a friend introduced me to a three-part course called the Landmark Forum. It sounded like a powerful program and just what I was looking for, so I started the course earlier in the year. I gained a lot from it, including improved relations with family and friends, and being more comfortable in my own skin.

However, the main gain is that the course led to the **CREATION** of a community project, and it was obvious to me that I needed to complete this project that my dad started more than 10 years ago.

So it's thanks to Landmark Education that my dad's book will finally be realised. And if the stories that I've received are anything to go by, I really believe my dad's simple idea about sharing our experiences will make a difference in people's lives and help bring about a more tolerant society.

EXPRESS

A poem by Edel McCormick

Destiny lies in hands with insufficient knowledge
Incapable of moulding a definite image
Puppeteers which, through ignorance are blindfolded
A distracted mind attempts to focus on present hardships
Which eventually are of little consequence
The selfish fears of others
Numb the only fragment of confidence
To lead the life which so desperately wants and needs
to be lead
Concern for those involved
Steals any chance of self **EXPRESSION**

TRUST

by Mona Quinn

My dear Martin,

To say I was thrilled to bits when I got your letter this morning is putting it mildly. I love you with all my heart, as I do all my children, grandchildren and great-grandchildren.

No, Martin, I was neither sad nor confused when your dad told me.

Let me tell you a story. When I was about 13 or 14 there was a man in Blackrock who was the most likeable guy I ever met. He was so funny. He could act the clown so well. This he did every Sunday.

In those days, Blackrock was thronged with people from Monaghan and Cavan. He was a gay man, and with the money he made going up and down the village every Sunday, in a few summers he made enough money to build Blackrock Chapel. Jim was a lovely man, and I'm sure God is rewarding him now.

Please don't look on me, Martin, as a saint. I have made

mistakes, too. As P. Sharkey told me many moons ago, "I will be a while on the landing", but if I get that far, I can wait.

Martin, you are a wonderful person, and Edel was too. You have no idea what her death cost me; I thought I would have died along with her. Every day I ask her to help me cope. I have her photo beside my bed, and I have no doubt she is helping me.

I know lots of gay people and they are all very nice. Who knows why God made gay people? You can be sure He has his reasons.

Now, Martin, if you can make a story out of this lot, you are indeed very clever. As a matter of fact, I sincerely hope you can read it. It must be years since I wrote a letter, but as I said before I was not shocked. We all have to put our **TRUST** in the Sacred Heart - without him there would be nothing.

It was wonderful hearing from you this morning, and I look forward to seeing you in August. May God bless and take care of you and bring you home safely.

I love you so much, Martin,

Gran

P.S. Peter, your dad, was like a son to me. I simply adored him.

WISH

by Finbar Travers

I first met Peter when both of us had a very happy event in our lives - the birth of our new beautiful daughters; Sarah-Jane (to me and my wife Margaret) and Edel (to Peter and Anne). The two girls were born two days apart in Drogheda Maternity Hospital. There was great excitement and happiness in both families during this time.

Peter was a first cousin of my wife Margaret; I spent time with him and I was very impressed by him, for he was a thoughtful and kind man, a real gentleman in every sense of the word.

He gave me a lift home from the hospital back to Dundalk and I thanked him. He said it was no problem and that maybe I'd be able to do him a favour one day... and here I am, 35 years later, writing a story for his book!

Many years went by before Peter and I met again. Margaret and I had been invited over to his home to have a talk about our children, Sarah-Jane, Edel and Martin, who had all bravely told us they were gay.

We all agreed how proud we were that our children had the courage to tell us, and we understood how very difficult this must have been for them. As all good parents should, we love all of our children unconditionally, but, to be honest, we had fears about their futures. Life can be difficult at the best of times, and being perceived as different could attract discrimination and worse.

Margaret and I had known about Sarah-Jane for longer and so were more comfortable with the situation. Peter and Anne had not had so much time for things to sink in and seemed to have deeper concerns than myself and Margaret. In any case, the main thing I remember about that conversation was how proud we were of our children for following the feelings in their hearts and not being too afraid of not fitting into the so-called "norms" of society.

That meeting with Anne and Peter was more than 10 years ago. Peter and Edel are unfortunately no longer with us. Martin is happy and has a successful career abroad. Sarah-Jane is living a full and meaningful life, after having serious health problems of her own.

Ireland has changed and things are much better compared to the days when I was young. But discrimination and prejudice still exist within some institutions in our society, though fortunately not in the more enlightened ones. I hope these changes for the better continue until homophobia is a thing of the past.

As a father of a gay daughter, I can only say that our lives have been made much richer by having a gay child.

Throughout the years I personally have gained an insight and greater understanding of our world and the diverse world of the gay community. Long live the diversity of life that exists in our natural human world! I just **WISH** for greater understanding for gay people who do not want to be seen as different because essentially they are not different. They are just the same as the rest of us, trying to live our lives as best we can.

LEARN

by Margaret Travers

My cousin Peter has achieved what he set out to do. Here we are sitting around our kitchen table with our family, talking openly about gay issues.

As a mother I have honestly never had a problem with my daughter Sarah-Jane being gay. She is part of me. I love her and my other children unconditionally. She is strong, funny, challenging, interesting and is always rescuing someone. We have **LEARNED** a lot from her.

Sarah-Jane was a happy child, but as a teenager she was unsettled and seemed troubled. She stopped confiding in me, and I knew something was going on. Her dad and I began to worry that she was ill or that something awful had happened - when I put the pieces together and realised that she was gay, to be honest, I was relieved! I thought, “Is that all?” I told her that I knew she was gay and that it was no problem. I wanted her to know that her dad and I were on her side, that she could talk to us about anything, and most importantly that we loved her.

Of course, I had my concerns. Lack of education and understanding leaves some people ignorant about gay issues. Unfortunately, some people think if somebody is not able to conform to the "norms" of society, there is something wrong with them.

I still have fears for my daughter in this world. Life at the best of times is difficult, and being seen as different can sometimes be dangerous. But I worry about all my children, their health and their happiness. I don't see my children's sexuality as any more important than any other aspect of their lives. It's just one of the many things that make them who they are, and I love them for who they are.

Before I got married and became a mother, I lived in London for a while. Some of my work colleagues and friends were gay. It didn't matter to me – it was none of my business. I like people because of their personalities and good character; their sexuality is irrelevant.

When I read or hear something negative about gay people, it annoys me. There are so many important things in this life with which should be concern ourselves, and other people's sexuality is definitely not one of those things. It seems that some people, when they think about gay people, just think about sex and sensationalising it; when they think about straight people, they don't think that way. It's so hypocritical.

From what I have seen, being in a gay relationship is about love, commitment, friendship and sharing your life with someone of the same sex. How can anyone have a problem with that?

All the gay people I have met are very supportive of each other, probably because they know what it is like to be treated unfairly and to need help. They are more open, understanding and accepting of others. If they were running the country, it would be a much better place.

COMMUNICATE

by Sarah Jane Travers

In October 1977, my mum and Anne shared the same labour ward, and Edel and I were born within a couple of days of each other - so we met at a very early age!

However, the first proper conversation I had with Edel was more than 20 years later, in the drop in centre of Dundalk Outcomers, a social and support group for gay, lesbian and bisexual people.

I started going to the drop-in centre when I moved back to Dundalk in 1999 (after living in Germany for a couple of years). Having a connection with the centre made being gay in Dundalk a lot easier. After a year, I joined the Outcomers committee and started doing voluntary work in the centre. One evening when I was on duty, Edel called in. I knew her to see. She was tomboy-ish and alternative like me, and I always knew we had something in common! We went on to become good friends. We would always have a good laugh and proper chats.

During that first conversation we realised we were related. My mum and her dad were first cousins.

Working in the centre, I'd heard that Peter had approached Dundalk Outcomers to discuss setting up a support group for parents of gay children and that he was hoping to write a book on the subject. Working on the helpline, I would often receive calls from worried parents, and I knew gay people of all ages who were having difficulties dealing with their parents, so I knew it was needed.

A couple of months after Edel and I had become friends, Peter approached my mum and suggested that she and my dad come to his house sometime to discuss "the situation", i.e. their gay daughters. I remember my mum and dad telling me about it and how they really didn't get what the big fuss was, but then they were well used to the whole gay thing by that stage.

Like a lot of gay people, I knew from an early age that I was "different". As a child I was quite a tomboy; I hated girlie stuff and thought my sisters were really weird because they liked dresses and dolls and not normal stuff like football and karate!

Mum and dad always encouraged me to be myself, so I had a happy childhood. However, during my early teens, I became unsettled and anxious. I had crippling crushes on girls and zero interest in boys (unless they wanted to play football with me!). I thought I was going insane and I couldn't tell anyone.

When I was 15, I met a girl and fell head over heels in love. After seeing how I was around this girl, my mum picked up on how I felt, and one night when I was sick (and all vulnerable and needing my mammy!) she saw her chance to bring up the topic. She said, "I know you are gay and I just want you to know that it is not a problem. Your dad and I love you no matter what and you can talk to us about anything".

Being 15, I didn't fully realise the significance of hearing those words. Like most teenagers (gay or straight), I was having a tough time with my parents, arguing about being allowed to stay out late, etc. and I was convinced that they were trying to ruin my life! Of course all that they were really trying to do was look after me.

At 19 I moved to Germany to study, and went on to experience all the highs and lows that life has to offer. After Germany I lived in Dundalk and then finally settled in Dublin, but I always stayed close to my parents.

The older I got, the more I understood what my parents have done for me and my siblings, how a lot of the time they would put our needs before theirs to ensure our happiness. They worked hard together to make sure we felt we could always **COMMUNICATE** with them.

Thankfully, that first girl I fell in love with felt the same and we started a relationship. I was on top of the world, but keeping it all a secret from everyone was very difficult. Throughout the years I gradually came out to friends and the rest of my family. Knowing that my parents knew and supported me made telling others so much easier.

I know now that though my mum and dad had no issue with me being a lesbian, they had concerns about how I would be treated by people with homophobic views. My parents never expressed this fear to me and were always positive about the situation, which made me positive, strong and not afraid to come out to others. Thankfully I have never directly suffered any homophobic abuse – maybe it's because I am confident and clearly proud of whom I am or maybe I have just been very lucky.

I remember Edel telling me when she was first diagnosed with cancer. Our family was no stranger to the disease, but I couldn't believe it. She told me that if I ever had any health concerns, to get them checked out as soon as possible because she had waited too long and the cancer had already spread by the time she sought help.

Shortly after Edel passed away I started having chronic headaches and feeling unwell. Remembering Edel's advice, I sought medical help and was eventually diagnosed with a rare form of blood cancer. That was four years ago and my life has dramatically changed, mostly for the better.

Now I know what really matters in life and what does not. In a lot of ways accepting this chronic illness has been a lot more difficult for me and my parents than accepting my sexuality. I find coming out as a sick person much harder!

I miss Edel and often think about her. We were born within days of each other, in the same place, into the same family, both lesbian and both affected by cancer. The whole gay thing seems so insignificant when compared with illness and the prospect of losing loved ones.

For as long as heterosexuals get together and make babies, they must accept that there is a chance those babies will be gay, and that as parents their child's sexuality should be the least of their worries!

A child doesn't choose to be gay and a parent can't choose whether or not to support their child, they simply have to - that is part of being a parent. I know that feeling unconditional love from my parents gave me the confidence to be true to myself. No matter what happened I knew that my family loved me and would always be there for me. That provided me with a foundation on which to build a happy life.

I love my mum, dad and the rest of my family dearly, and I thoroughly enjoy spending time with them. They have always been there for me and I will always be there for them.

Like everyone else, I did not choose my sexuality. Of course, sometimes I wonder how different my life would be if I was straight, but the reality is that I'm not and life is too short to pretend to be something I'm not.

By being true to myself I have always been able to live my life with the freedom to love who I love and to be loved in return for being the real me. What more could a person ask for?

UNDERSTAND

by Bernardine Quinn

In 1993 the then-Minister for Justice, Maire Geoghegan Quinn, fast-tracked legalisation decriminalising homosexuality through the Dáil, after the mother of a gay man asked the minister how she would feel if her own son was gay and criminalised.

The love of a parent is often the difference between a young gay person making it or not. We sometimes underestimate the desire of a child to meet the expectations of their parents, but often we don't think about the parent needing to meet the expectations of their kids. Some parents make a very conscious decision to make sure they are what they need to be, to parent their children well.

In my line of work, I never thought I would ever have needed to know anything about the support of parents for their children. I was working to support gay people.

One of my very first consultations as a support worker for gay and lesbian people was from a straight man. He was a father of not one but two gay children: he wanted, needed, to know how he could best support his kids. He had a lot of questions he needed answering, ranging from "Why me?" and "What was my role in their turning out to be gay?" to "What can I do? What do they need?" Big ask from someone who had never had such a conversation with her own parents.

We just had to put our experiences out there: he asked the questions as a dad, and I answered as a daughter. I realised then, and many times since, that in order to do some parts of this job you didn't need a lot of expertise: it's about sharing of experiences, being honest and open to hear, and trying to **UNDERSTAND.**

I am sitting writing this in a week that marks a phenomenon that we do not fully understand, for which we do not have answers. However, what we do know is that it has taken so many gay lives from us. It's Suicide Prevention Week here in Ireland. I can't help but think of the many LGBT people who took their own lives because of the lack, or perceived lack, of support from the ones they loved.

I can say in confidence that the love, understanding and acceptance of a parent to let their child spread their rainbow wings and look on with pride at how they fly is the secret to keeping our gay kids safe and helping them grow into the people you know, and they know, they can be.

Peter was a dad who so wanted not only to see his kids meet their potential, but wanted to know how he could support that. He wanted to make sure his children had a positive, safe and equal shot at whatever they wanted to achieve. But more than that, in a time when it was not cool to do so, he wanted other parents to support and talk about their gay kids and to celebrate the gift they had been given.

Now, with the untimely passing of Edel to breast cancer, it is so obvious the gift she was to us all.

I tried to think of a way to end this letter, and I think the best way to do it is to say that I think Peter's dream is becoming a reality as more and more parents come to our door wanting the same questions answered.

As more and more young gay people "come out", I see a change in Ireland. I hope wherever Peter is today, he sees the same, and he sees how his son not only met his potential but far surpassed it. That he sees the road to full equality for LGBT people gets easier to travel.

I have never forgotten Peter's visit to our centre; it has enhanced my learning as well as, I hope, his.

ASK

by Tony Hanna

Peter was a staunch member of our weekly prayer group, a quietly spoken but perceptive analyst of life and people. He was a deeply spiritual man, humble and gentle in his conduct and speech. The twinkling eyes betrayed a lovely sense of humour that was both self-deprecating and mischievous.

Yet underneath the quiet, unassuming face that Peter presented to the world, there was an inner courage and mettle to deal with great challenges. Peter may have been small in stature, but he was resolute and unflinching when it came to matters of principle or justice.

When Peter **ASKED** to meet with me to discuss something of importance to him, I assumed it might have been something to do with some help in his spiritual life. The topic he brought to our discussion was surprising and somewhat challenging for me, but it was profoundly traumatic and deeply personal for him.

Peter had come to me asking me to include a workshop for "Catholic parents of homosexual adult children" in a forthcoming conference which my community, The

Family of God, was hosting in Dundalk under the theme 'Family at Crossroads'. His discovery that two of his children were homosexual had almost overwhelmed him when he first encountered it. Yet he faced it steadfastly and looked at it through the eyes of love and compassion and he found peace.

"Peace I leave with you; my peace I give to you; not as the world gives do I give to you. Do not let your heart be troubled, nor let it be fearful" (John 14:27).

Ultimately his deep faith helped him to live with the turmoil and many unanswered questions. He also felt called to a mission, which was to highlight the trauma of parents caught in the backwash of deep emotions of confusion, compassion, guilt, anger, regret, love and hurt, and to find some mechanism whereby they could support each other.

Peter also felt called to ask the church to look again at its response to homosexuality. Ireland was a very different country in the 1990s, and the subject of homosexuality was more than a little taboo.

As I recall, we had already agreed on the conference program and had invited speakers, including our local auxiliary bishop. When I brought it to the Council of the Community for its consideration, there was fear and a great reluctance to get involved in a topic that could prove very embarrassing and perhaps damaging to the reputation of this fledgling community, in the eyes of the church.

Peter's proposed workshop was a potential time-bomb and one that was considered very risky to undertake. And yet there was the witness of Peter himself! He had come to us as a father who loved both his homosexual children. He was coming to the church asking for help in how he should respond. There was nowhere else to go at that time.

He knew there were other parents like him struggling to make sense of it all, parents who knew the church's position and who wanted to be loyal, obedient and faithful, but parents who also loved their homosexual sons and their lesbian daughters whose lifestyles were at odds with the teachings of the church.

Frankly, I was not sure where to begin, but I was convicted by Peter's sincerity and his own faith life. I knew his pain and the internal turmoil through which his faith was trying to navigate.

I agreed to set up the workshop. I asked a well-known moral theologian who was known to be sympathetic and liberal in his views to conduct it. I balanced this approach by asking a lecturer in Moral Theology at the Pontifical University, Maynooth (now the president), to act as chairman.

We wondered if anyone would turn up to the workshop. We feared it would be contentious, that the press or media would get wind of it and that there would be a hullaballoo. None of these things happened. The workshop was excellent, well attended and hugely helpful to those who participated.

I know Peter was delighted, and it encouraged him to consider becoming more proactive in setting up a self-help group for parents of homosexual children. I think his proposed book was one of the initiatives that flowed from the conference.

I have little to add other than to record my own appreciation of a life well lived; a humble, dedicated family man who, in his own quiet way, raised questions for the church to consider as part of its pastoral ministry.

The homosexual question is complex, sensitive and difficult, and the church has a responsibility to hold fast to sound doctrine. She is also called to marry that responsibility with compassion for those whose lifestyle is not compatible with church teaching.

Peter walked a personal tightrope between these two poles. He was a good man in the truest sense of that simple but profound accolade. May he rest in peace!

REASSESS

by Jimmy Woods

Dear Martin,

As you probably already know, I don't understand homosexuality, and possibly never will. This is not because I have closed my mind on the subject, but because I am heterosexual.

The only homosexuals I would have seen in my life would have been when I lived in Scandinavia in the early 1960s. The ones I saw were exhibitionists, camp and generally not nice people to know – but remember, I only saw them from my own perspective.

When you 'came out' - I think that is the correct term - I had to stop and **REASSESS** my views on this matter, for you were a person I had known since your boyhood years; somebody I respected and loved to meet as you socialised with my own children, your friends. You are surrounded by people who love you, stand by you and accept you for what you are - a good, decent human being.

Your father Peter realised this was not the case in other families who found themselves in similar circumstances, and he wanted to do something about it. He was a man who believed in the goodness of God, and in the knowledge and belief that God created us all equal. This statement will be questioned by people looking for answers - and rightly so. Peter believed that we were created in love and God would sustain us in that same love, but we had a part to play in it as well.

When something is beyond your understanding and people are involved, we concentrate on the people. For they are the same as us all, just wanting to lead good lives, be happy, to love and to be loved.

Jesus said, "Love one another as I have loved you". That is why you are loved so much by your family and friends.

Regards,

Jimmy

SHARE

by Joan Woods

Dear Peter,

Your **SHARING** with us on Thursday night was such a revelation and so inspirational that I just had to put pen to paper. I don't know how you feel, but I do know with God on your side the situation you both find yourselves in at the moment will undoubtedly bring yourself and Anne close together in love.

Your love for your children goes without saying, and our love for Martin from our very first meeting is evident. Martin has a certain aura about him that one couldn't but love, and our love for him is unconditional. Irrespective of what Martin would do, that love I have for him would not diminish.

I thank God for Martin's friends and how faithful they are to him and I've never heard a derogatory remark passed about him and his sexuality. They just accept him as Martin, their friend.

The situation is indeed very difficult to comprehend, and I know all sorts of thoughts, especially for his future, compound Anne's and your mind. The main thing is to remain focused on God and live for the now.

The trip to Australia will be a real blessing for you to see Martin in his own environment. The plans he has for you both show how much he loves and appreciates you and needs your support.

Martin will never be anything to me and Jimmy but a perfect gentleman, and I do mean gentle in the nicest possible way. His concern for me when I was in hospital was paramount, and I knew that from Seamus.

We are so fortunate to have become so involved with Martin's parents and we thank God for that grace. It is always a pleasure to be in your company - you are so lighthearted and so spiritual - the highlight of my week!

Life is not easy and was never meant to be - God did not promise us a trouble-free journey, just a safe arrival and eternal happiness for all of us. None of us know what tomorrow will bring - we live for today and put our complete trust in God and the Holy Spirit.

God bless. All my love,

Joan

LISTEN

by Siobhán Leonard

When Martin was about to tell me his news, he rang me at work in Bank of Ireland to say he wanted to meet for a drink and a chat and I couldn't refuse.

"Interesting," I thought. I used to walk into work in my tracksuit and change into my uniform when I got there, so needless to say I didn't fancy going out unless I was in 'going-out' clothes. Looking back at the silliness of it all - I was worried about my attire, and Martin was about to explain a life-changing event!

We went for a drink in The Temple Bar. I think I had two sips, and Martin said, "Let's get to the point - I'm gay".

I don't think I was shocked or even reacted; then again it had to sink in. I do remember thinking, that's the missing piece about Martin. I couldn't pinpoint what that missing piece was, but now I had a word to describe it. Call it instinct or a woman's intuition, but Martin being gay clarified a lot for me. It completed Martin as a person, albeit it's only one aspect of him as a human being.

I suppose I was (as was my sister and brother) brought up in a fairly sheltered family and community. Being gay never really entered the equation, though I'm sure we knew people who were, but obviously not openly. It's only now looking back with a more broad mind, I can recall times and situations that are more clear to me now.

Martin's coming out, I suppose, meant he would be looking for something different (to my mind) in a relationship, and also would have a different circle of friends while hopefully keeping his old ones. Martin is still Martin, with all his faults and failings as we all have, the one we love, respect, and with whom we have a laugh.

My message to anyone - be it mother, father, son, daughter, brother, sister, relation or friend – is that if you feel or think something is not as it should be or perceived as "not normal", chances are you're right. Be open to **LISTENING** to them and trust your instincts. It will be different for everyone, as is the relationship to begin.

I remember one night living in Phibsboro in the early 1990s, and Martin came round for a visit. Fair City (a soap on national TV) happened to be on, and the main storyline at the time was about a gay couple. Ironically, one of the actors (Alan) was from Martin's school; he may even have been in his class. As we were watching TV, I said, "Hold on, I want to see this" as the actors were about to kiss. I reacted with a "yuk" or an "eek", as one would.

Martin obviously knew he was gay at this point, or at the very least knew something was not as "perceived normal" with his sexuality. I'm not sure what he felt at the time or even now if he remembers, but for someone going through such a dilemma in their own minds, I'm sure it didn't help with everyone he loved around him having negative feelings towards gay people. What must it feel like when in your friend's mind and eyes "this is not so normal", but to the gay person "this is so normal"?

Then again we live and learn, and maybe it's to be more aware of people's feelings and try to be more in tune and think before you speak or react as it could have a detrimental effect on someone else.

As I now have two children, I'm wondering what I would think or feel if they told me they were gay. I know deep down that it's not what I would wish for them as it's an upward struggle to be recognised and accepted as different. Having said that, it's not a disease, and no matter what life throws at them it'll be a battle to a certain extent.

Finally, let's not forget your sexuality is only one aspect of a person, it does not define you. It's important to let everyone get on with their lives and not get too distracted or bogged down on the sexuality of a person.

One of my favourite lines from the movie/musical Moulin Rouge is as follows, and so in whatever shape or form it takes: "The greatest gift you'll ever learn is just to love and be loved in return".

LAUGH

by Fiona Breslin

We were all living in Dublin at the time, and over a week or two Martin made a number of attempts to organise to go out for dinner with my sister Siobhán and myself.

It didn't appear that all three of us were going to be available to go out for dinner together for some time, so in the end Martin decided that the two of us would go out for dinner together and he would hook up with Siobhán at another point.

We went for dinner to a restaurant in Dublin city centre - my memory is of being in a dark restaurant with a hushed, basement-like feel to it, possibly Mexican. We sat at a small table for two along the back wall of the restaurant, me facing outward into the restaurant and Martin facing toward me. The tables were very close to each other, too close – I clearly remember that. You know the way there is a very thin line between making maximum use of the space in a restaurant to fit in as many customers as possible and then just simply overdoing it so that you feel slightly uncomfortable being so close to the people beside you.

There was a couple to my left, having what seemed like a very romantic candlelit dinner. “If only those two weren’t sitting so close,” I imagined they were thinking. We, too, were at a candlelit table, so I am sure we appeared similarly – a happy couple having a romantic dinner out together – talking and **LAUGHING** lots, which would be the norm for our time spent together. We talked for a little about this and that, and then Martin said he wanted to tell me something. I had the specifics of this moment of time etched accurately in my mind for many years – the exact wording, in fact, but as it happens the details have become vague throughout the years.

My recollection is that Martin started by saying he had already shared this with my brother Séamus (his closest friend) and had wanted to tell my sister Siobhán and myself at the same time. But the way it had turned out, that he was now going to be telling us individually, was probably for the best since we are very different people.

He then went on to tell me that he was gay. He most certainly didn’t tell me using those exact words, but I honestly can’t remember what he said – I just remember feeling an overwhelming sense of emotion and started to cry. To this day I don’t understand why I cried. You cry when you are sad, happy, even angry, but all I can think is that it was an instant, pure, emotional response – the kind that comes on so quickly you don’t even have time to guard yourself against it - or anyone else for that matter – not having time to weigh up your reaction, measure it, or choose the appropriate response. So there it was – my raw reaction at a candlelit table in an intimate restaurant in Dublin city centre.

Martin knows I am a big softie, so I am sure this reaction did not come as much of a surprise, and he immediately acted like the gentleman I know him to be and started to console me. After some time, I noticed the couple who were sitting to my left had gone extremely quiet and were now just looking at each other. It was clear to me that this was not a lovestruck gaze between them, but more, "Are you hearing the conversation between the two next to us?"

I looked intently at Martin and subtly nodded to my left. At that very moment the two of us burst out laughing, both realising at the same time what the couple must have deduced after earwigging on our conversation.

They obviously presumed, as I had done of them, that we were a couple having a romantic meal together and then, what do you know, 'the boyfriend' (Martin), like a bombshell tells the girlfriend (me) that he is gay and I, 'the obviously devastated girlfriend who had been totally oblivious to this fact' bursts out crying with 'newly arrived out of the closet boyfriend' trying to console me.

I can only imagine what they then thought when we both instantaneously burst out laughing so hard – they must have just thought we were nutters!

Martin went on to explain many things, including the fact that he had known he was different from a very early age, say four or five; he had been careful when consciously choosing my brother Séamus as a friend in secondary school because he seemed sensitive and kind; he had been with a few girls but it never felt right; and he had been in denial for many years.

He also told me how it came to be, that on the night his parents and he talked about the fact that he was gay, it also came to light that his younger sister Edel also felt she was gay. This added a whole other dimension to the story. I truly felt for his parents. I thought this was very, very unusual that two siblings were both gay and told him so, but he informed me that it was not at all that unusual.

I remember feeling sad - why, I can't quite articulate, perhaps simply feeling for him, for the struggle life must have been so far, the fact that he would not be getting married or become a father (not in the conventional way, anyway), the struggle life was going to continue to be for some time. Maybe forever!

How was I to know how it was all going to turn out for him, how he would cope, how people would treat him? Wouldn't there always come a time in his work life, social life, etc, where he would have to state the fact that he was gay, pronounce his sexuality? How unfair was that - having to inform people (to whom you were not close) of something so intimate. Straight people never have to make that kind of pronouncement because we are the 'norm'. I fundamentally felt that a difficult life lay ahead of him.

I had known Martin since he was 13, since his friendship with my brother Séamus started in first year of secondary school. I knew he didn't seem to get that many snogs, shifts - whatever you want to call them - but in some way in the back of my mind had put it down to the fact that Séamus was perhaps better at chatting up the girls and he was a great dancer, so that also helped with the ladies, I'm sure. Because I had reasoned this out, Martin coming out was a total surprise for me – a shock. I did not see it coming one little bit.

Among the emotions tinged with sadness was a kind of giddiness, and I openly said to Martin, "I can ask you all those questions about gays that I have always wanted to know". That's how I felt, too – a door had opened into another world. I could ask honest, straight questions without offending someone and could get better informed about how it all was in the gay world... not from a camp, dramatic, effeminate gay man, but from my solid, loving, gentle friend who I loved dearly.

It seems that friends of ours who had only met Martin for the first time in the year or two before he came out automatically presumed he was gay – he wasn't camp in any way, but they just 'knew'. I explained to them that perhaps if I had met Martin in his early twenties, as they had, that it may have been obvious to me, too. But I had known him from a young boy of 13, and thus my perception was clearly very different. They couldn't believe that I had not had any inkling of his homosexuality, and some laughed openly about this which made me feel, I remember, foolish, innocent, gullible and totally naive.

Betty, the mother of Orlagh, a friend of ours, when told by Orlagh that Martin was gay, very caringly said, "Oh, I hope no one hurts him". Orlagh's take on this was that her mammy had heard of men being beaten up because they were gay, and she feared for Martin. I always thought that it was lovely that she was so worried for his wellbeing. Here was a middle-aged Irish Catholic woman, and this was her lovely, caring reaction on hearing about Martin.

I am so happy for Martin that he came out and allowed us to know him in a more whole sense. I can only imagine the pressure and weight that was on him and the lightness he must have felt as he revealed himself little by little to all close to him. I think it is one of the bravest things anyone can do – to show more of themselves - and for someone who is coming out as Gay, all the more courageous.

I dedicate the following piece to my wonderful friend Martin because I know in coming out, in the way he lives his life and finally in taking on the completion of a great piece of work his dear father started, is liberating others.

"Our deepest fear is not that we are inadequate. Our deepest fear is that we are powerful beyond measure. It is our light, not our darkness that most frightens us. We ask ourselves, who am I to be brilliant, gorgeous, talented and fabulous? Actually, who are you not to be? You are a child of God. Your playing small does not serve the world. There is nothing enlightened about shrinking so that other people won't feel insecure around you. We are all meant to shine, as children do. We were born to make manifest the glory of God that is within us. It's not just in some of us; it's in everyone. And as we let our own light shine, we unconsciously give other people permission to do the same. As we are liberated from our own fear, our presence automatically liberates others."

A Return To Love: Reflections on the Principles of A Course in Miracles by Marianne Williamson.

CONTEMPLATE

by Séamus Woods

Knowing Martin as a school friend and as a travelling companion during our teenage years, it has to be said that yes, I was certainly taken aback when he told me he was gay.

Martin's qualities that I knew him to possess and which led us to be friends in the first instance were that of a true, thorough, genuine and solid character. This, therefore, made his revelation more sincere and exact. This is not to say that humour didn't get us through this time, as it did in our school days. At the time of his disclosure I remember ordering a few more drinks as I let the news take hold.

The following few weeks were strange, I suppose. Many situations in the past now made sense, as Martin recounted these times to me and why they occurred as they did. I felt Martin wanted me not necessarily to ask lots of questions, but he desperately needed me to talk and talk on the subject when in actual fact what I really wanted to do was just let it be.

I think he found that much harder initially than I did,

endeavouring to come to terms with the fact of him being gay. Why is it difficult for people to come to terms with the fact that at certain times in life you just need time? Did it take a major effort on my part to prove something, or did I need to mark out what my acceptance criteria was, even though I didn't even know what that was myself - did I accept it or would I ever?

Inevitably, I wondered how his experiences in life were more than likely going to be different to what I was intending to hopefully experience. Relationships, marriage, children, holidays, socialising, perspectives and overall the path that lay before him as opposed to the one that I assumed he would follow.

We socialised as a mixed-gender group, and maybe to a large extent this made things much easier. The demarcation lines could be more easily drawn because when Martin wanted to be his true self he socialised with a different group, but when he wished to be part of our group he decided to join us. We knew him throughout the years and therefore still treated him exactly the same.

I continued to behave in the same way as I had always done with the acknowledgement that there was a large part of Martin's life that appeared different through this new revelation. Indeed I had a better understanding of where Martin was coming from and the reasons for many of his viewpoints.

There are decisions in life when we make a choice or decide preference. When someone does not have a choice or is born a certain way, they have to deal with the hand God has dealt them. This can indeed be very tough at times, but isn't this the courage that should be commended, not condemned? This applies to anybody dealing with a major aspect of their lives contrary to the apparent norm. The perceived image of homosexuality and stereotyping certainly distorts this issue, and to a large extent the relationship you have with a friend to whom this issue pertains.

At the end of it all, I know that Martin desires a companion and partner in life, like many people. Is this what many of us look for and hope that it will lead to greater contentment in life? Yet we may not want this, and still be as contented in life. But these things are our choice. My understanding of being gay, through being a friend of Martin, is that being gay is not.

As a friend of Martin's, I never knew whether I did the right thing as a friend since he came out, and that is the challenging part. Did I give him enough space, did I try to engage with the idea, did I allow him to show me what his world meant to him, and did I leave him be when he needed it? Where do I draw the line? Where should I draw the line? Is there a line?

These are the grey areas that I probably found difficult throughout the years. The resistance to being open as friends, the barrier Martin would agree he had put up, was that due to a large extent to his sexuality or because that was his way? Subsequently, I found that I avoided discussing the areas that pertained to Martin's gay world, and I assumed he never wanted to chat to me about them. They were for his newfound friends.

When an aspect such as this is such a part of someone's life, it inevitably consumes them to a large extent. Socially, emotionally and physically. Where did I or should I stand for that matter? To what degree are you part of their lives, simply because I've known him as a friend for so long? Or do I let him have his life aside because his circle is unique?

As life moves on, I think we are more truthful about what is going on in life. I think in the earlier years, so much time for Martin was subsumed with "the scene" and how he fitted into the overall culture.

I knew Martin for about seven years before he came out and, yes, they were the formidable years, but we have continued that friendship for the past 20 years.

Through time and viewing aspects of life in a more **CONTEMPLATIVE** way, I think many situations develop clarity. I am in a different place in life, and in many ways with different priorities and perspectives. Hindsight is great, of course.

I am saying all this as a friend and, like many things, I think it would be very different as a parent, on whom it has a greater impact to a greater extent because of the innate relationship between parent and child.

At the end of the day, God loves us for being us - my summary of it all and how I genuinely feel is that: "To love, and be loved, is everything".

OPEN

by Barra O'Donnabhain

I've always known that I was gay, even before I had the language to express that. I've also known from an early age that this was something that was problematic, even dangerous.

In Ireland in the 1960s and '70s, this was true of all things sexual. There was little or no public discussion of sex or sexuality in general, only veiled, euphemistic language that was full of sin and shame. And that was only for the heterosexual, missionary-position, contraceptive-free, within-marriage stuff!

There was certainly no space to voice the concept of same-sex attraction. Yet there were tantalising suggestions that this existed out there somewhere, even if only on the road to perdition!

I remember as a 10 or 11-year-old, hearing older kids talking about someone being "one of those", a term that was accompanied by an action involving a limp wrist. I wasn't quite sure what this meant, but I knew it was not something you wanted to be. Kids, of course, hate being ridiculed, and like most, I just wanted to fit in (of course

I've since learned that adults, particularly straight men, are also terrified of ridicule and being different).

As I got older and heard more details, I suspected, dreaded even, that I was indeed "one of those", though I hoped I would grow out of it. I had good reason to be hopeful as other than the dictionary, the only book I could find at home with the word "homosexual" in the index was Dr Spock's Baby and Child Care, which mentioned that children went through passing phases of same-sex attraction.

As time went on, though, the hope that I would grow out of it began to wane and a certain dread kicked in. Why would you willingly be "one of those", when the only role models were men whose very names were bywords for ridicule: Larry Grayson or Mr Humphries in Are You Being Served? This was not helped by the fact that most of what I knew about sexuality was gleaned from other kids at school, some of whom had accurate information, but others were way off the mark!

There was very limited information imparted at home, and while the clinical mechanics of reproduction were discussed at school, this was done in the context of a Catholic retreat, so it was all delivered in a very traditional, conservative view of human relationships that left no space for deviation from an idealised, Catholic 'norm'.

The creeping realisation that I was different didn't provoke any crises until I was in college. With hindsight, though, I can see that the need to hide my huge secret influenced my behaviour long before that. I was always rubbish at anything that involved kicking or hitting a ball, and in my GAA-obsessed primary school that was not a good place to be. Ironically, as my teen years progressed, I became estranged from those to whom I was increasingly attracted: guys my own age. I felt that my secret was safer if I avoided their company. This structured my friendships in a way that followed me into adult life.

I had a few girlfriends (OK, two!) in my later years at secondary school and one in college. I really hoped with each one that this was the relationship that was going to turn things around and make me 'normal'. Of course, that didn't happen, and in college, as my peers started to pair off, I felt that it was harder to hide.

Unfortunately, college also showed me the hostility of the world to gay people. During my first or second year, the Students' Union had a referendum on whether or not UCC (University College Cork) should have a student gay society. It was defeated in a secret ballot among the students. That 'adults' should be conservative was understandable, that kids my own age would also think this way was devastating.

Things got worse a year or two later when a brave young guy called Cathal Kerrigan was elected as president of the students' union. When he stood for election, people did not know he was gay, but he made it quite clear afterwards and proposed establishing a college society for gay and lesbian students. The university administration refused to sanction it. Not a surprising reaction from officialdom at the time, but it was the reaction of my fellow students that was more disturbing.

One incident a little time after this was like a nail in a coffin for me in terms of my attitudes to Cork and

UCC[3]. This was the year of the hunger strikes in Northern Ireland, and a general meeting of all students was held to discuss the matter. Cathal Kerrigan, who chaired the meeting, started by saying that there was a query about the Students' Union's attitude. Well, on the mention of the word query, the place just erupted into laughter. A queer saying query! What a laugh. A proud moment for the future leaders of Irish society, and a moment when one 20-year-old queer retreated further back into the closet and became increasingly desperate about the need to hide.

Some relief came soon after that as I discovered a pastime where I could hold my own with straight guys: drinking beer. This coincided with moving to a postgraduate program, and I was lucky to be in a department with a few other gays and lesbians, even though none of us acknowledged it at the time.

In my early 20s I think biology took over and I gradually moved from wanting to hide to wanting to get it on. Cork was a) a hostile wasteland, and b) where I was more likely to be recognised, so I turned my attention to Dublin, where I had a wonderful cousin and later my brother.

After a few months of pondering and "will I? won't I?" agonising, I answered an ad in In Dublin magazine. Many of these ads were scary in a number of different ways (highly sexual, desperate), so the one to which I was drawn was very down-to-earth and about friendship. I took the plunge, and while I did not find a boyfriend, within a few weeks I had a circle of gay friends. For the first time ever, I felt like I really belonged.

[3] I now live in Cork again and work in UCC and I'm glad to say things have changed.

The Dublin scene in the late 1980s seems almost comical and quaint now, looking back on those times. There were a few pubs with predominantly gay clientele and, thanks to David Norris and others, the Hirschfield Centre.

To realise after your entire life that you are not alone is a very powerful experience, and I felt that I had a lot of catching up to do in terms of growing up and being emotionally involved with another person. After a lifetime of hiding and denial, it was great fun with this new group of friends to spend 90 per cent of our time together commenting on guys. Much of the rest of our conversation was spent talking about who knows, who doesn't know and who will never know.

There were stories of guys who got beaten up or who were thrown out of home once their secret was out. That was one thing that I knew would never happen to me. I was lucky to be born into a family where I always knew that whatever happened, it would be dealt with in a way that would never involve expulsion! On the other hand, I absolutely cringed at the thought of the process. I came out to my siblings one by one and got positive reactions in all cases.

My parents were the last to know. By then I had lived in the US for five years, where I encountered a much more tolerant society than what I had left at home. By the time I moved back, it seemed a silly waste of energy to keep this big part of me from them. So I sat them down and said there was a discussion we needed to have! All went well. It was one of those situations where, afterwards, I wondered what had all the fuss and dread been about.

My parents and my brothers and sisters have been great

allies, and they wholeheartedly embraced my partner Adham when I met him in 1996. That family support has been really important to us both. Our nieces and nephews do not remember a time when we were not a couple, and I hope that has a positive impact on their lives.

I met Martin early in the summer of 1995, and we dated for a few weeks before making a smooth transition from boyfriends to friends. The night I met him, Martin mentioned that his younger sister Edel was also gay. In one of those 'small world' moments, I realised that I had already met Edel a few months before. This had happened when I met her friend Owen in a club in Dublin.

He mentioned that he and his lesbian friend had missed the last bus or train home to Dundalk. So they ended up staying in my flat, Owen in my room and Edel on the sitting-room couch. She was very quiet and didn't say much that night or the next day. I suspect that she was a bit embarrassed about playing gooseberry!

Edel was only 18 at the time and so diminutive that she looked younger, so I was surprised when Owen told me that she was **OPEN** to her parents and had a girlfriend in Dundalk. Surprised and probably a little bit in awe that someone so young was so brave in her dealings with the world. It had taken me a lot longer than 18 years to get to a similar place. Owen also mentioned that Edel had a gay brother and that their sexualities had caused some distress within the family.

So when I met Martin, I was curious to know how this had all played out at home. It's very common for gay people to exchange their coming-out stories, and my curiosity was driven by the experience of navigating the process in my own family. Like many gay people,

I had spent a long time asking 'why' and 'why me', so Martin and Edel's stories brought me back to the question, was it nature or nurture?

When I lived in the US, I knew two sets of identical twins who where both gay, and that for me pointed to nature. Nature was definitely my preferred answer because nurture raised the spectra of fault and blame: an added burden that I did not want to land on my parents.

Nowadays, with the benefit of hindsight, questions of nature or nurture seem a little simplistic. I view sexuality now as a spectrum with boundaries that are defined by the prevailing culture. As our society has become more open and accepting of difference, it has become easier to voice same-sex attraction and to act on it.

It's probably difficult for younger people to realise the anguish suffered by so many around issues of sexuality in the not-so-distant past. Up until relatively recently, Ireland was a harsh, hypocritical place where people who were different in any way had two options: shut up or get out. Throughout the years I have met plenty of people a little older than I am who repressed gay feelings, got married and just hoped it would go away. It's difficult to contemplate those lives of quiet desperation and the damage inflicted on spouses and children, but this was our society's preferred option: never mind the misery, outward appearances were what mattered.

For the individual, a life of pretence was preferable to being a queer, a lezzer, a pervert, a fag, a homo. For many, the only context in which you heard anything at all about gay people was in taunts like those. In that atmosphere, homosexuality was totally beyond the pale. Your options were stark: hide and conform or become a pariah and object of ridicule, derision and hate. Not surprisingly, many chose to check out of our society. Tragically, for many that meant self-destruction in its various forms.

One of the things that struck me about Martin in the mid-1990s was how important it was to him to be open about his sexuality: to his family, in the workplace, and with his friends. He wanted people to know the real him, he did not want to hide or pretend. That takes guts.

I have always felt that the caricature of gay men as sissies is particularly unjust because the reality is that it takes balls to be openly gay, even today. Imagine then what it took, say, in the 1950s? We owe a huge debt to men and women of earlier generations who had the courage to be themselves. We can speak openly of the love that dare not speak its name because they dared.

I see Martin and Edel in that tradition of brave individuals, like Cathal Kerrigan and David Norris, who were not willing to compromise their own personal integrity. Their desire to live open, honest lives might not seem now like a lot to ask, but that has not always been the case.

Edel's short adult life as an openly gay woman was a form of quiet activism, a refusal to lie down in the face of adversity, a trait that she demonstrated to the end.

ADMIT

by Séamus Mallon

I met Martin some time ago, in fact just a couple of years shy of 20. Scary thought how fast time flies.

Back then I was seeing Claudio, a Brazilian guy living in Dublin, and he invited Martin and a few friends over to his place for dinner. From then on I would see Martin out on the gay scene in Dublin, and after I broke up with Claudio we both ended up in a relationship for two years or so.

Admittedly, it was very casual to start with (on and off a number of times from what I remember), and looking back on it now it probably wasn't a match made in heaven, but at the time I was happy and it worked as well as it could. We had the guts of a year in Dublin together before moving to Sydney, where we lived together for a year before we broke up.

While we were together, we both talked about our families. I remember Martin talking fondly about his parents and how close they were. I don't really ever remember him talking about them arguing or not really getting on. I know that they went through some difficult times when they found out that his sister was gay and then also Martin. I'll admit I felt slightly envious of his family, so my overriding impression of them was always a positive one.

I remember meeting Martin's parents when we both went to Belfast for a weekend. I can't remember if we stayed in Martin's house overnight, but we did visit his parents and they were pretty much as I expected - both very nice and welcoming at the time. It must have been hard for Martin's parents to meet someone with whom he was going out, but if it was, they definitely did not make me feel in any way uncomfortable.

I am from a much bigger family than Martin's - one brother and five sisters. My home life was generally good, but there were difficult times. Growing up, money was always a struggle, and caused some tension in the family.

I found it difficult to relate to my father, and as a result our relationship was not as good as it could have been. He was from a different era, he seemed to live his life in the past, and was as happy as could be doing manual work out on the farm from morning to night. My mother didn't involve him in the financial side of running a farm and feeding a family, so he never had the stress of that knowledge. That was for my mother to bear and, for a small part, also included me as my mother would often involve me in any decisions involving the farm and money.

'Coming out' came relatively late in life for me. I was 22, and I say late in life because a lot of people, particularly young people today, seem to be able to deal with their sexuality at a much younger age. This makes me feel very envious because when I look back at my life, particularly before coming out, I have a sense of regret that I wasted so many years. That said, they say you are a product of your experiences, and I guess maybe if I had come out earlier in life I might not be the same person that I am today.

From a very early age I always knew I was different than other kids, a feeling that is very common with most gay people. Way back then I didn't know what that difference was, but I knew it was there. I was a shy kid, and I think that shyness was one of a number of reasons why it took me so long to deal with my sexuality. In school I was bullied a bit but not overly so, and I was lucky that I didn't stand out as being effeminate so I was never specifically picked on for being gay.

I didn't have a huge amount of friends in school, but the ones I had (unknown to me) have pretty much all turned out to be gay. It would have been great to have known this back then, but even if I did, I'm not sure what I would have done with that information. My mind was much closed to the whole gay thing, and though I knew I was different, I was years away from having the courage to **ADMIT** to myself I was gay.

From the age of 13, I hoped the attraction I had for other boys would pass and that I would be normal, but it never did. I knew that this was not something that I could ever tell anyone, and whenever these thoughts would come into my mind I would quickly push them away.

At the beginning it was not too difficult to ignore any gay feelings I was experiencing. In my early teens they were not as strong as they would eventually become, and I had lots of other things to keep me occupied. I had made up my mind that I would do whatever I had to do in order to be normal, and I wouldn't allow myself to ever consider the possibility that I might be gay and what that would mean for me.

Unlike today, there were little or no gay role models in the media apart from the stereotypical gay man, limp-wristed and camp as all hell. At the time pretty much the only gay representation on the TV was Julian Clary, and though he was a funny guy, he was not someone with whom I could ever Identify, which only increased my resolve to never admit to being gay.

My first three years in school were not too bad. I had a few close friends and some girlfriends, though we never did much more than kiss and hang out. However, my last two years were not so good. I became more introverted as I struggled to cope with my dark secret. I had some close female friends, but I did not want to be known to have only girl friends as this would draw attention to the fact that I was different. At times during those years I did feel very lonely and, looking back now, I definitely do feel sad that I missed out on enjoying my school days more.

I can't help think that things would have been much easier for me if gay people and gay issues had a much bigger presence in the media back then like they do today. The more normalised homosexuality becomes, the less of a big issue it is.

I had a very strong resolve not to admit to being gay, but a lot of that was based on fear and ignorance. I was definitely not very well informed and truly believed that gay people were dirty, sad and effeminate people who were destined to a life of loneliness and discrimination. Not a very attractive proposition, and certainly not a lifestyle that would encourage me to ever come out and admit to myself that I was one of them.

It blows my mind sometimes when I think of all the talk we have today about gay marriage, and that back in Ireland you can now publicly declare your love for your partner by entering into a civil partnership with that person. Granted, a civil partnership is not marriage, but when I was a teenager I didn't even know that gay people could have relationships, let alone ever be this close to being able to get married. And I am absolutely certain that in most countries gay marriage is only a few years away. How far we have come!

After school I went to college. Ironically, that college was in Dundalk, Martin's home town. I still pretended to be straight, but life for me was getting harder, in the sense that my self-esteem and self-confidence were on a downward spiral. For me, not having the courage or the pathway to deal with my sexuality was having such a negative impact on my life. Coming out as being gay is a long process, but you are 99 per cent there when you can acknowledge to yourself that you are gay and that you are going to finally deal with being gay. I was still a few long and difficult years off doing this.

For the latter half of my time in my last year in college I had a girlfriend called Marina. She was a very good-looking girl and I was amazed that she was interested in me. Unsurprisingly, there was no sexual attraction for me, but I was happy to have her as a girlfriend, as it helped make me feel more normal. In my head I felt that having sex with a woman might somehow cure me of being gay, but it never happened as she wanted to wait until she was sure I was the one for her.

After college I moved to Dublin for work, and not long after I ended the relationship with Marina. By now I was finding it harder and harder to cope. I knew I was gay, but still couldn't come to terms with it. I knew it was not fair on Marina to pretend I had feelings for her.

My self-esteem was at rock bottom at the time. I decided that I would end the relationship and never go out with another girl again. I was sure she would understand and quickly realise that she would be better off without me. I broke it off with her over the phone and I remember being really surprised that she was so upset. I had convinced myself that I was someone not worth crying over, so I was not prepared for this. I couldn't give her a clear reason as to why I was breaking up with her, and to this day I am pretty sure she does not know why.

I obviously couldn't tell her the real reason. I could still barely admit it to myself, so I definitely couldn't say it to her. At 21, I was at a very low ebb in life and on the verge of falling into a deep depression, but luckily for me things were about to change.

Not long after breaking up with Marina, and thanks to the encouragement of a work friend, I ended up joining a sports complex. Due to a combination of not having many sports options in school, coupled with a lack of self-confidence, I had never really done much sport or physical activities. However, from the first day of getting my membership, I became addicted to working out at the gym. I took up swimming lessons, learned to play squash and badminton and at one point even took up step-aerobic classes, though this was short-lived because of my lack of co-ordination!

Looking back now, it is clear to me why I became so obsessive with filling my time with physical activity. The busier I became, the less time I had with my thoughts - which meant I could avoid having to deal with my sexuality. This ended up being a good thing as through working out and taking up sports, my body started to change in a positive way. I quickly put on some muscle mass, my confidence started to increase, my mood improved and I finally felt ready to accept that I was gay and deal with my sexuality. The only thing was, I didn't know how.

I know that this might seem strange but it never occurred to me that there might be phone helplines that you could ring that would give advice and guidance on how to deal with being gay. I was very ignorant about what support there was out there to help. Instead, my first gay experience resulted in some action I took after reading an article in the Sun newspaper about a private members' club for gay people. I remember reading this and thinking that this must be what gay people do, go to these places to meet gay men, but then lead normal lives at all other times. It made perfect sense to me at the time. Nobody would ever know, or tell anyone, as everyone would be in the same boat as you.

That was how I had my first physical contact with another man. Definitely not the best place for this to happen, but through a lack of knowledge on my part it seemed the only option available to me. So as I headed off that night, with a few strong drinks beforehand to settle the nerves, I took the plunge and took the first step on a journey that truly changed by life.

I won't go into details about what happened that night, but I will say that being with another man felt totally right for me. I met my first boyfriend that night, and from then onwards everything changed. I didn't come out overnight, but the most important step for me was admitting I was gay to myself and deciding that it was now time to deal with this fact. And this is what I finally did.

Initially I thought the best way to deal with being gay was to leave Ireland and live somewhere where nobody knew me. At first I thought America, but after realising it would be impossible to get a visa I decided on Australia. However, through the help of a counselor I realised this was not the answer, at least not until I got my finances in order. This counselor made me realise that I would have to come to terms with being gay in Dublin, and over time that is what I did.

Before coming to terms with my sexuality, I always thought that I would never come out. But when I did, I have to admit it was the best thing I ever did. Since coming out, my life has exceeded my expectations in every way. Not that this would have been hard, as back then I didn't have many expectations from life. But, really, the peace of mind that I have got since coming out has been something I could not put a price on.

Admittedly at first I led a double life until gradually over time I was able to tell more and more people I was gay. Coming out for me was being able to admit to myself that I was gay and that I was going to do something about it. Telling people I was gay didn't happen straight away, but it did slowly start to happen.

The first person I told was my college friend Caroline, who had moved to New York. My first trip overseas was to New York to see her, and then Florida to see my sister. I had decided that Caroline was going to be the first person to tell, and then my sister. My plan was to tell both of them on my last day of being with them.

I told Caroline in Central Park, and it was probably one of the hardest things I have ever done. I was practically shaking and could hardly get the words out. For whatever reason Caroline laughed it off and thought I was joking. I was so relieved to have got the words out and thought that her reaction of disbelief better than rejection, so I didn't correct her at the time. Two weeks later when I got back to Ireland I had a letter waiting for me from Caroline. She said if I was gay she would be 100 per cent supportive, but if I was joking she would kill me the next time she saw me. Caroline was the kindest person I think I have ever known, so I should have known that she would have been there for me no matter what.

I then told my sister, which was a bit easier than telling Caroline, and every time after that it gets easier. But certainly the first number of times you tell people it can be hard and it can take a tremendous amount of energy. A good friend of mine used to say that every time he told someone he would be so mentally and emotionally exhausted that he would need to sleep for a week afterwards to recover.

My journey definitely was not easy, and I do feel sad that it took me so long to come to terms with my sexuality. But it is what it is. Coming out was without doubt the best thing I have ever done. It will also probably be the most difficult thing in life with which I will have to deal.

It is great to see the world changing, and hopefully over time coming out will not be such a big deal. Gay people will be able to get married, have children and be treated no differently from everyone else. This is what I hope, but also what I believe will eventually happen; you can see it slowly happening now.

CONFIDE

by Rosie Hoey

As a young child I was happy. I came from a loving and happy family, and never felt that I wanted for anything.

But I'd say even before I was 10 I started getting very quiet and shy, and even though I was popular enough, got on good with school work and sports, I still loved to get home to my room and close the door on the world. As time went on I became more introverted, and though I excelled in life, my inner world was in turmoil. I started to question myself. Am I normal? But then what is normal?

I seemed to be lacking self-esteem, confidence and I didn't understand all of my emotions. I came to the conclusion that I felt nothing. Numb. I can live with that ... and believe my numbness was the easier option for me to fall back on, for many of the years to come!

So on I went with life. Then the realisation, 'Oh my God, I have feelings for girls', no, that's impossible. It goes against everything I was brought up to believe in. It's wrong, it's dirty, and above all else it's a mortal sin. How can I sit in church on a Sunday with my family knowing what I know! I'm a sinner. I started praying to God to take these feelings away from me; to please make me normal.

My friends like 'getting off' with boys. Why can't I? I mean, I like boys, I enjoy being around them. I'm a better footballer than most of them. I spend more time with boys than girls, but when I kiss them I don't feel anything. I don't like it. There must be something physically wrong with me.

Then one evening I was out for a spin on my bike and I saw my friend Edel's bike on the side of the road. She was in the ditch. She had been to a friend's house, and they drank a bottle of whiskey. I took her back to my house to sober her up as I knew my parents were out. After a while we really started talking, and I told her about my feelings for girls. She said she felt that way, too, and had actually kissed a girl. We laughed about it because deep down we both knew about the other without it being said.

We then started reminiscing about conversations we'd had years before and having boyfriends but not really enjoying kissing them, but that's just what you do. 'Lesbian' wouldn't have been in our vocabulary back then. We were both popular and fitted in easily with the boys because we played football with them and got out of school to go to matches, which none of the other girls did.

After that night such a weight was lifted from my shoulders and I had a **CONFIDANT**, who had been my friend from childhood until the day she died, and even now I still talk to Edel in my own wee way.

Even after that night I still seemed to be getting more and more introverted, so much so that my parents noticed that something was wrong and got help for me. I started seeing a psychiatrist and a counselor and was put on medication for depression. I saw the counselor for a good while before I told I thought I was a lesbian. And that only came about because one day I was in my room crying uncontrollably and my aunty, who was visiting home from England, asked me to tell her what was wrong.

I told her I had feelings for women. She said it might be just a phase as I was still young, but if it wasn't then it was still OK. So my aunty came with me to my next session with my counselor, and I just let it all out. My feelings, my shame, my fear, and that I didn't want to be like this.

At the time I was becoming good friends with a girl and had quickly developed deep feelings for her. Of course I was too scared to do anything about it, but one night we were out and she kissed me. And it happened again and again. I loved it and it felt so right. Finally I had a physical connection with someone and it had done something positive for me. Of course I told Edel straight away and she said, "You see, I told you you'd like it. It's lovely, isn't it?" And yes it was lovely ... it felt normal for me.

I had planned to tell my parents, but the sudden death of my father put an end to that idea. I just couldn't let my mam deal with it on her own. I thought she'd feel ashamed of me and wouldn't want me any more. So I told my older sister. She said she thought I might be and said, "Welcome to the club". She'd been in a relationship with a woman for years. I couldn't believe it. The two of us are gay!

Edel had told me that her parents had found out about her brother and then her. I was envious at the time of Edel, thinking her parents know and are OK with her, she doesn't have to hide any more. But in further conversations with her, she had said it was good that they knew, but it wasn't as plain and simple as that. But I so wanted to tell mam ... but not yet!

I started going to the odd gay disco with Edel, but deep down I was still in turmoil and very confused, and petrified of people finding out about me. We still continued to go to our local pub, too, but I felt we were looked down upon, especially by the lads we were friends with growing up in school. I was still going out to pubs and clubs with another friend, getting off with lads, torturing myself trying to be 'normal'. Living two lives, and not quite fitting in with either.

Edel asked why I was doing it, and to tell my friend about the real me. So I did. She was shocked and didn't take it too well at first, and I thought, "Fuck it, I'm going to lose a good friend because of what I am". But thankfully that wasn't the case, and she remains a friend to this day.

After another year or so of torture and having the feeling that I wasn't getting anywhere in life, I decided to move to England to train as a nurse. My dad, whom I was missing terribly and still do, had always wanted me to have a career and not be dependent on anyone. I was drinking a lot, too, which was going to become a big problem for me later. I wanted a new start. I was now ready to go.

After two days in England, I befriended a lad, on my course at university, who was gay and he took me to a club that night. I was speechless. It was packed full of people. Openly, men with men, women with women, like it were the most natural thing in the world. Which of course I now know is perfectly natural.

It wasn't too long before I was like a child in a sweet shop! I was out most nights partying and having a ball. I spoke to Edel regularly and she visited a few times. I told her I was living my life, no one was judging me, and I was being me.

I started coming out to those around me at university and the girls with whom I was sharing a house. I was making loads of friends, gay and straight, and it didn't matter where we all went out at night.

It was coming towards the end of my training when I met and fell in love with the woman with whom I was to spend the next three and a half years. I had secured a good job, we were living together and we were happy. Her family knew and welcomed me into their family. This was my normality.

I wanted to take her home on holidays with me, and she wanted to meet my family, to see where I was from. But then the dread, I'll have to introduce her as my girlfriend.

My brother was coming home from Australia, on holidays so that was when I planned to take her home. He was delighted to see me so happy and said he didn't care that I was with a woman. Another brother said he didn't give a shite, while my other brother was a bit shocked as he had no idea, but soon came round.

Luckily they all liked her and all was well. She attended all the family parties and weddings. I'm pretty sure the relatives knew, but nothing was ever said to me.

It was now time to tell mam, who was in hospital at the time and very sick. I was afraid she might die not knowing the real me. I told her that my 'friend' and I were more than just friends; that we were together in a relationship and living together. To my surprise or shock, she asked if I was happy. I said I was. Her reply was that as long as I was happy, that's all she wanted for me.

So I headed back to England, ecstatic. Mam still loved me. So life went on, job going well, everyone at work knew I was gay and didn't care.

After three and a half years, the relationship ended. I was devastated. At the time I wasn't well. My depression had come back with a vengeance, and my drinking was spiralling out of control. I was hospitalised for a time and really struggled. Who could blame her if she'd had enough? I can see that now, but couldn't then.

So back came my old friend numbness, only I'd gradually found throughout the years another way of achieving that. Oblivion at the bottom of a bottle and any other drug that worked (a whole other story!). I didn't have to feel anything, push those feelings and emotions away, numb again. I was a mess. I started sleeping with men again and women still. Trying to change who I was. The longing to fit into the world again.

I received a phone call around this time that my brother in Australia was coming home. He had cancer and was dying. So I decided to take time out and come home to nurse him. Edel was very sick at the time, too, and they both died within six months of each other. There are no words to describe how I was feeling. I tried to get back to work, but it was obvious to all I wasn't well. I needed help and I needed to move back home to be with my family.

Months before Edel died, she sat me down and said, "Look at me, I'm dying of cancer. I don't want to die, and you are killing yourself. Please get help". I couldn't. I wasn't ready. I needed my coping mechanism for a while longer.

But then the time came and I was moving back home for good. I got help. I went to a treatment centre to dry out, followed by an after-care program and counseling. I started seeing my old psychiatrist again to get the depression under control, and get my mental health back.

I'm home a few years now. It's been a tough journey. I'm lucky to have met good friends in my self-help group who love me for me. One friend told me the good thing about getting sober and mentally well is that you get your feelings and emotions back, but the bad news is that you get them back, too. I now understand what he meant.

The difference is I can cope with them today in a healthy way. I don't have to hide and feel numb. I have peace of mind and I'm comfortable with me. I have a good life now. I haven't found the woman of my dreams yet ... but I'm pretty sure Edel will send her my way when the time is right. Well, I keep asking her to, anyway!

FEEL

by Meela Bradley

I met Edel when we were still so young - kids, really. We had clicked and caught fire almost immediately, and heaven help anything or anybody in our path. She was my first love, the love of my life.

I remember the first time I visited her family home. It seemed so alien to me, so very different to my own. A beautiful house on landscaped gardens filled with tasteful furniture, family portraits and Catholic pictures. From the very beginning I admired this beautiful family haven where there were very clearly two loving parents providing shelter and comfort for their children.

I soon met Peter and marvelled at his gentle spirit and kind manner. Over time, the house became familiar to me and again I was struck by how 'normal' it all seemed. When I met Anne, I could **FEEL** her tension and apprehension, but I now know she was a mother trying to protect her family. It was only a short time since two of her children shook her world to its core.

The truth is I never felt comfortable there. I felt I was chaos in a peaceful serene setting, intruding in this calm and measured life that Peter and Anne had made for themselves.

In writing this, I got to think about how chaotic Edel must have felt in that home. This is no reflection on the welcome I was given. It was always very warm, but I could see Peter struggle with what was going on. He liked me, he chatted and laughed with me, and I know that he adored Edel. But I saw the conflict in him in small moments between banter and chats; a faraway, thoughtful look, perhaps trying to make sense of this situation, perhaps trying to tally it with his own beliefs and his ideas of how family life should be. I can't speak for him, but I sensed that careful contemplation from him.

Edel confided that in this home she always felt like a misfit, and after she came out, a disappointment. As her feelings of disconnection grew, so, too, it seemed, grew the distance between Edel and her mother Anne. I think Edel felt that she had broken her father's heart, but at the time could feel only resentment from her mother.

Edel often spoke of her feelings of estrangement from her family. She felt at times that they had nothing in common with one another, nothing to say to one another since her 'secret' was told. It saddened me to think of this beautiful family scattered and disjointed.

Patience is something we all exercise when dealing with family at some time or another, and I believe that, just as in any family, the problem was not knowing how to communicate properly, to honestly talk to each other and be vulnerable with each other.

I secretly wished Edel could sometimes just say, "I'm afraid of all this. I don't know all the answers and I need a little guidance and reassurance", instead of being such a hard nut. I secretly wished I could have whispered to Anne, "You have the most beautiful girl in the world as your daughter. Nothing has changed, she's still your baby and she still needs a cuddle". And I wanted to reassure Peter that I respected him, his values, his beliefs and that I meant him no harm.

I am, to my abhorrence, a people-pleaser. I'm getting a little less pathetic as I age, but it's still there in my core. I don't like to rock the proverbial boat, I follow rules, I avoid conflict at all costs and against all my logic and reasoning, I like to conform. In this spirit, feeble and weak as it is, I implored Edel to be kinder with her parents – to respect how difficult it was for them.

Poor Edel, she had so many of her own emotions with which to deal, so many thoughts to process, and I was asking her to be mindful of those of her parents, too. It's something I feel bad about now.

I met Anne many years later as a 'grown-up' – she regularly met a friend of hers for lunch in a restaurant at which I worked. We had not seen one another in a very long time, and were now interacting on a totally different level.

I was in a straight relationship at the time, had matured and been manicured, and it was very clear that this made Anne much more comfortable around me. She seemed to approve. The people-pleaser in me was thrilled!

In this newfound easiness between us, I toyed with the idea of asking her all about how she felt back then when Martin and Edel came out, when I invaded her home, when after I had gone and butch lesbians and fabulous gay men became part of her world. Did she have any regrets? Would she change anything now looking back?

The coward in me prevailed. To this day I haven't sat and had a truthful, open conversation with Anne.

Edel adored Therese as her older sister, was grateful for her kindness and understanding. I often felt a small pity for Therese, who, in her own way, must have felt put out or even left out. Edel always spoke of Martin fondly and with real affection. He had paved the way for her in some respects. I know that Edel felt that she had an ally in the family, someone who was like her. I think it made it a little easier for her to deal with the disappointment she felt from her parents.

I remember one night Edel, Martin and I went out in Dublin to a gay club, had a dance and plenty of laughs – overall a great night. What struck me was how cheerful and uninhibited Martin was. He had always seemed so formal when I met him at the family home, quite a world away from this warm, laughing, happy young man.

The real tragedy for this family turned out to be cancer; first Peter, then Edel. I often wonder if they somehow look back on those times, 'the coming-out era', as carefree and easy in comparison. I wonder if they all found a new perspective in light of cancer and its catastrophic shadow. This is not to belittle the magnitude of coming out – it is, of course, a life-changing event.

Gay is not the end of the world. Death is the end of the world. Until then, we have the chance to shift things, make changes, adjust, fight, accept, love, learn, understand, communicate – all the things that we as human beings are born to do. It is a challenge, for some it is a confrontation, when one member of a family comes out.

For Peter and Anne, after two of their children came out, I'm sure it seemed impossible, and yet life went on. For Therese, Martin and Edel, it was family life and all the reality, frustration, laughter and madness that that entails.

This book is only part of the story of a very ordinary family – a loving relationship between two good people that developed into a family of loving people. It is not a fairytale. Why do we all still strive for a fairytale?

Too often, people make instant and sweeping generalisations and judgments when they hear the word gay. I do not identify as gay. I do not identify as straight. My sexuality has always been very fluid and transient to me – I like what I like. I've never really thought of it as something that defines me; it's a private thing I feel no real need to share with others. This will anger some members of the gay community as I do nothing for their cause being non-committal and oh so vanilla, but I, too, have my place in the grand scheme of things.

Long ago and far away, a tiny little lady bowled me over. Absolutely floored me with her wit, charm and soulful eyes and I was smitten – like never before, and never again. Time passed with the ebb and flow of her presence in my life, but her pull was always there – calling me, inspiring me, challenging me and consoling me. When she died, when she was senselessly taken from us, I thought I, too, might die. Bereft and set adrift in emptiness, I tried in vain to conjure that pull again, to hear her voice in my head, to feel something, anything that would reassure me she has not left me.

Isn't this grief? Isn't this love and loss and human anguish? Gay, straight or other, can't we all identify with that?

EMBRACE

by Helen Brassil

My parents are Catholic. I was never forced to attend mass and I escaped from having any religious ideals pushed on me. I was sent to a non-denominational school.

I have both my parents to thank for this. My mother had very little time for nuns, having suffered them all through her schooling. However, this didn't stop her from going to mass, or from praying to Saint Jude while I was off gallivanting around Europe 'finding myself'. I saw religion as a familiar base people turned to when all else failed - not so far from the truth, I guess.

As I came of age and realised I was gay, the last thing on my mind was, what will God think? I was more concerned with the extreme lack of other gays around me, which made me feel isolated, as if coming from Cooley wasn't isolating enough for me!

Edel was my first gay friend. She truly was a lifesaver. I remember Martin came out, then Edel. In a way, I shadowed their experience to avoid doing the deed myself. It was like we opened the door for others like us, to come and hang out. This was a brave thing to do in Dundalk in the '90s. We made other gay friends and partied our summers away. We were finally out. Granted, we were armed with quarters of vodka and Buckfast, but we were 'out' nonetheless.

I have fond memories of Dundalk then. We shared some good times, and it didn't feel like we were being judged (I'm sure the curtains were twitching and tongues were wagging, but we weren't bothered). Anyway, being bisexual among our age group was all the rage then, which helped the situation significantly! I hadn't officially 'come out' at this time. I still didn't feel the need, I guess.

After my leaving certificate, I moved to Dublin and left small-town life behind me. I quite enjoyed being different - I was anyway, as there was a touch of anarchist in me. I **EMBRACED** it. It wasn't something I fought.

However, I was a little concerned with the heterosexual-to-homosexual ratio. I now realise this was a lot to do with people's fear of coming out. And this was mostly because of an island that was stiflingly Catholic, a country where church and state were joined and decided what people should, and shouldn't do. Oh God.

Neither myself, nor Edel took any of that nonsense to heart. It was like a Father Ted sketch, ridiculous to the point of hilarity. All you can do is sit back and laugh, and do the complete opposite to what you are being told.

It took me a while to come out to my parents. I didn't think they would get it, and I didn't want to upset what already was quite a detached household. I do remember downing a half-bottle of Jameson and slurring it out at some point in my early 20s. No one was surprised.

In fact, my brother just called me greedy! That's the strange moment where the child ends up educating his/her parents about things. Initially, this is a very odd feeling.

I am now engaged to an amazing woman, and perspective has come into play. I guess my parents are both at ages where they are lucky to be healthy and active. My mother always says, ''Your health is your wealth''.

My sexual orientation, like anyone else's - gay or straight - is so irrelevant in the grand scheme of things. Love is relevant. Being happy is relevant. Having witnessed Edel and Peter go so prematurely, this rings true time and time again. Life is short.

When hearing of Edel's cancer, I rang the family house phone. Anne answered, and I soon realised Edel had a huge battle on her hands. The odds were certainly stacked against her. None of it made any sense, cancer never makes any sense.

I met up with her, and we had a few drinks. She was physically exhausted. I did what I could to raise some money for her trips to South America by running a couple of music gigs in Dublin, but nothing seemed like it was enough to make a significant difference. I remember feeling quite helpless.

We watched Titanic together a few weeks before she passed away. One of the final scenes where the ship sinks slowly slowly into the ocean, Edel said, "Jesus, that would be an awful way to go''.

She was a true friend, and Peter, a true gentleman.

TELL

by Owen Kavanagh

Coming out was probably the most difficult and most courageous thing I have ever done in my life.

As a child I not only felt different, I was different. I always wanted things that other boys did not want - my friends were girls; I played dressings-up with my mother's make-up and clothes; Wonder Woman was my idol; I asked for dolls not footballs. So I was ridiculed by classmates and neighbours, taunted and alienated. Life was not easy.

My teenage years were even worse. At secondary school the mockery became cruel. At puberty my feeling of being different intensified. To appear to be one of the lads, I had several girlfriends, but by my late teens I was sick of trying to conform.

Coming out in a small town was not easy. I was lucky though to find security and support in friends facing the same problem, one of whom was Edel.

I met her through a mutual friend. She was a warm, open and caring person. We spent many a night chatting into the wee hours. For me, she was part of our family. This gave me confidence and a newfound sense of happiness.

Eventually I felt strong and ready to **TELL** my mother about my sexuality. I have always had a close relationship with her and felt she would understand, but she lost it! She said I was going through a phase, I was being ridiculous.

I went to bed distraught. What could I do now? I decided to write a letter to try and describe how I felt.

The following day I was resigned to having to go on as before. My mother came home from work, she too, was distraught. She said she couldn't get her head around it, that she would need some time to think.

It did take time, but the dialogue had started.

After that day, I felt so much better. My family now loves me for who I am. Unfortunately not every gay person's family is as understanding.

REMEMBER

by Jaime Nanci

I wish so bad that I could **REMEMBER** how we met. I have tried and tried to recall, but it's all such a blur, my teenage years soaked in cheap cider.

When Martin asked me to write something about Edel, my initial response was a sad but certain 'No', mainly because I genuinely have such a bad memory I didn't think I could do her justice. But with a little coercion and much soul-searching, I felt it would be remiss of me not to put pen to paper, to at least make some effort at remembering the amazing, huge impact this absolutely tiny dyke had on my life.

So who cares how me met? The important thing is that we met.

Dundalk in the mid-1990s was not the gay metropolis it is today! And yet four of us found each other; as my mam says, "Water finds its own level".

We were quite the gang. Two baby dykes and two baby gays. We were out and proud at 16, and no one really bothered us. We had a big circle of oddball friends, we went to Ceasar's indie disco every weekend, moshed around drunk on two pints, swooned over boys and girls, went back to one of our houses and all passed out in the same bed. Nothing and no one could touch us.

I remember Edel. A tiny beautiful gentle girl who sometimes people mistook for a boy. Leather trousers; I didn't know they made leather trousers that small. She always had a smile on her face, and such a filthy laugh.

I don't know how we met, but she was there. As close as sisters. She even makes an appearance in my sister's 21st/debs/family history video, which I just recently watched.

I remember the last time I saw her in The Spirit Store. It had been years. Maybe 12 or 13 years. We'd had a stupid teenage falling-out. I was 'in love' with our mate, made up some story to make him jealous that backfired, and we fell out.

Summer ended. School ended. Life took me out of the town. And I rarely went back. So it was pure chance that we bumped into each other in the pub. I knew immediately something was wrong. She was fighting that shit hard. But she gave me her beautiful smile, we hugged, laughed about what had come to pass, how foolish we were to let childish games end our friendship. Shrugged off the past and picked up almost where we left off.

She told me she was going to Mexico for some intensive treatments, but she was adamant she wouldn't be beaten. I guess the illness got her, but I think this collection of stories shows that Edel wasn't beaten. She is still smiling on all of us; I can still hear that filthy laugh of hers.

Things have changed so much for gay kids since Edel and I were running around Dundalk together. I married the founder and CEO of the national LGBTQ youth organisation BeLonG To three years ago, so I'm immersed in the ever-evolving face of LGBTQ youth life in Ireland.

It's amazing to see these changes sweep across the land. Youth groups and drop-ins have been set up in over 15 locations all over the country, so kids don't have to travel for five hours from Donegal just to get two hours every second week where they feel like they aren't "the only gay in the village".

I think about Edel pretty much every day now. The girl she was seeing, when we were teenagers, coincidentally works at my gym. When we stop to chat, we share a laugh about what wild things we were back then, and then we smile a bit and get a little maudlin thinking about wee Edel. Then one of us will remember something silly that she did, or said, and we will be off laughing again.

CELEBRATE

by Kevin Callan

The first time I ever saw Edel was at a non-alcoholic teenage disco in the Fairways Hotel. Studio Eight ... till late.

I was 13 years old. I had been allowed to go to this disco once my older brother David agreed to look after me. I think it was my third or fourth time there. It was all still new and exciting. It was early days for me getting dressed up in something I thought was cool, for being out and seeing what other kids were wearing. What music were they dancing to? How did one dance? I was terrified.

At the time I very much fancied girls. I had always fancied girls. I was beginning to notice boys as well, but I don't remember being completely conscious of that. At that point it certainly wasn't a concern. The biggest concern of course was the first time I shifted (kissed) a girl. Boys were out of the question at this point. When and with whom would I end up slow dancing? Would I make a total fool of myself? How exactly does one do it? Would I be any good? How much tongue is enough? I was terrified. Basically I remember that being the overriding feeling ... terrified excitement.

I had spotted Edel from the beginning. She stood out. She was small and cute, had beautiful eyes and was dressed totally differently to everyone else. She was wearing black jeans, big black biker-style boots, a combat/army style jacket or shirt. She had her hair shaved on the sides, an undercut, with her hair still long on top and tied up in a ponytail.

She was shocking. I mean it. Here I was, faking it until I made it, a country kid still figuring out what these cool townies were doing. I was shocked by her. I didn't know what to call it at the time, but I had never seen a girl be butch. And Edel was butch. She dressed like a little hardass.

Most of the guys there were dressed as ravers or in fashionable gear or whatever. The girls' fashion at the time escapes me, but Edel was dressed like an attitude-filled, grungy boy. I had never seen anything like it. I recoiled. I didn't know what to do with the image of her. I found it threatening. I didn't understand why. I mean, she looked edgy, yes... and I was in awe of the fact that her clothes spoke of coolness, knowledge and "fuck you-ness".

But I was threatened by the fact that she was a girl and looked like a boy. I guess I had quite a homophobic reaction to the sight of her, though I didn't quite know that either.

As the night wore on, I still hadn't had my first kiss. But I was pretty happy I had mastered dancing and was happily resting on my laurels. Edel and her friend Ruth were standing over by the DJ booth when Ruth strode over to me and asked me if I would shift Edel. I was mortified! Of course I was embarrassed because I had never kissed anyone before and wasn't ready for this brazen ambush.

But mostly I was mortified because I felt that Ruth suggesting that I kiss Edel was some accusation of me being gay, too. It's funny. I didn't know that Edel was gay from looking at her. I didn't know what to call her, she looked so alien. But I knew she wasn't like everyone else.

I had always been bullied for being gay, even though at that point I didn't even know I was, but I knew enough to know that being associated with the brazen Edel was a sure way to be singled out as different even more than I was already. I still needed to hide any sign that I was different.

Edel was not hiding. I've never really consciously acknowledged this about Edel until I come to write this now ... She was so courageous. She made no attempt to hide who she was. I shyly refused the offer of "the shift", and it quickly became apparent that Edel had had no part in the request. Ruth had done it to embarrass her and me as a newbie on the teen disco scene. And so I didn't speak to or really meet Edel until about two years later.

I had never fitted in. When I was little I was serious and shy. I was timid and didn't like to be boisterous. I didn't like doing things wrong. I was never athletic enough or strong enough and could never see the point in being competitive. I stuck out like a sore thumb. From an early age I was singled out for being a sissy, a woman, and as I got older, a faggot. I preferred hanging out with girls. I didn't like sports or the things that most lads did.

When I hit my teens I found the social scene. Fuelled by binge-drinking and the confidence it gave, I developed a whole new persona. I had developed likes for the 'cool bands'. I had figured out what clothes to wear and I was having a blast. There was drinking in pubs and in parks, smoking cigarettes, seeing bands, smoking joints, and basically pretending to look like I knew what I was doing.

I had also had a few girlfriends at this point and was pretty settled on the fact that I definitely fancied boys as well. Either by luck or design, the friends I ended up with were pretty open about talking about same-sex attraction. Among my close friends it was an acceptable part of our alternative persona.

While I continued to be singled out at school and in certain social settings, around my buddies I was comfortable with the fact that I liked boys. At least I could hide the fact quite convincingly because I genuinely liked girls, too.

On another fateful, fun and drink-fuelled night, I bumped into Edel again. This time the situation was much different. A firm friendship was born. I was that bit older (15 to her 17) and immediately recognised what we had in common. We were both different. I had just caught up a bit and begun to embrace my difference a little.

Edel, me and others formed a close alliance. We were all gay, bisexual or experimenting. We all liked music and we all liked to party. I was home. Finally I fitted somewhere. Finally I felt what made me different made me special - at least when I was around my friends, and key among them Edel.

Rights of passage such as school and college, first kisses and love, conflicts with parents and family. All of it was being experienced through a new lens, through the lens of friendships formed with people among whom I could be my whole self. Normal was a dirty word. I loved it.

Edel was out to everyone. It's not like she went around saying she was gay, but because she was unable to be 'girly', it was pretty obvious. I pretended to myself that everyone didn't know about me.

I knew Edel was out at home and that she felt pretty alienated from her parents about it. She didn't talk about it much in detail, but I do remember her being very angry. She was angry about their struggles with it. We, in the way you do when you're young, rolled our eyes at her parents' silliness that they just couldn't be cool with it.

Edel definitely reacted against it. Edel wasn't angry in her manner, but she was moody and frustrated. We had that in common, too. We had both been hurt by people's lack of acceptance of who we were. It had affected our acceptance of ourselves and our behaviour. Having Edel, with whom to navigate all this, made her my family.

My experience with coming to terms with my sexuality was a mixed bag. I was so fortunate that at a key point in my life I met Edel and others, so I had people to reflect back that what I was feeling and who I was, that

I was OK.

When I was 16 I sat down with my mother at the kitchen table. I had something to tell her. I said, “I’m bisexual”. She smiled and said, “I know that, pet ... and you fancy him and him”. (I have since settled on the gay tag, but I still believe that sexuality is a gray scale with preferences along it - men are my preference, so gay it is.) I knew my mother would be cool about it.

It was a huge relief. In my teens I had a troubled relationship with my dad, so I put off telling him for another two years. I told him by letter from the safe haven of University in England. He called me and assured me that whomever I loved I was always welcome in his home and that he was immensely proud of me. I was shocked at my reaction. I sobbed with relief. It showed me how afraid I had been of the potential of his rejection.

I can’t imagine how it must feel to be rejected by your parent because of being gay. It must have such a profound effect on your whole sense of yourself. Add that to the inevitable feeling of difference you would have felt among your peers.

Many of my friends have had bad experiences with their parents. I am so grateful I was as lucky as I was. All my life, up to that point, I had been told in one way or another by my peers that who I was, was not all right. I was not normal. That had, and still has, a profound effect on how I view myself.

With the benefit of adult hindsight, it is no coincidence, in my opinion, that a central activity among Edel and I, and our mutual friends at the time, was drink and drug abuse. We all drank to excess and continued to do so into our twenties. I can't speak for Edel, but my experience growing up as gay has definitely had a lasting effect that has taken some work from which to recover.

I have an abiding memory of Edel sitting on the edge of the pool table in one of our favourite bars. It sticks in my mind because it wasn't like Edel to get visibly upset. She was crying and confided in me that she felt that she would never meet anyone. She felt that as a gay woman in Dundalk she was unlikely to meet anyone. She wasn't sure what path her life was going to take, and for the time being she would be living in Dundalk. How was she ever going to meet someone? She desperately wanted the same experiences as I, or any of her friends could have.

At the time I secretly shared her fears. I didn't really know any other gay girls in our area who weren't already among our friends. Of course, we couldn't have been more wrong. Edel went on to fall in love and have great relationships. She was a big hit with the girls.

Recalling all of this makes me marvel at just how difficult it is being a teenager. We have all heard it said, but I've never realised it before. Edel obviously had a keen sense of how difficult these years can be as she began a career working with troubled teenagers. She was extraordinarily gentle, kind and wise.

Growing up has its challenges for everyone, gay or straight. Everyone, child or adult, wants a feeling of belonging. We want to feel connected and feel like we are loved. It is too easy for us all to find things that make us feel like we're not good enough and therefore don't deserve to feel connected. Not liking yourself for any reason is damaging, be it because you're gay or because you believe you're ugly or stupid.

Fear of not being accepted is part of the human condition and is not particular to gay people. However, there is a feeling as a gay person that you are at risk of exclusion because you are different. The fact remains that there are a large proportion of people who are afraid of what is different. Homophobia is one of a litany of phobias in our community.

It seems to me that we should teach our children to **CELEBRATE** what is different about themselves and others. It is through our individual differences that we are all the same.

It has been so good to be reminded of how blessed I was to have had the coming-out experience that I had. It is through my relationships with my family, my friends and lovers, through my relationship with Edel that I have learned to love and be loved.

SUPPORT

by Kay Callan

I first noticed Edel when she was very young, maybe eight or nine, in a coffee shop with her mum and gran.

I recognised an indefinable difference in her that I also saw in my son Kevin. She had a tomboyish look and she looked you straight in the eye. She wasn't a little pink girlie girl. She was small and pretty with very short curly hair. She had a stride that belied her small stature as she walked alongside her mum and gran.

I must confess I'm a people watcher and I was curious about her. I saw her regularly, especially during school holidays, as I attended that coffee shop restaurant daily at my break time.

Some years later when Kevin and Edel were teenagers, I got to know Edel through her friendship with my son Kevin.

One day while at work I received a phone call from Peter, Edel's dad. He talked about a project he wanted to start and said I might be interested in it. I arranged to meet him to discuss it. At this stage I wasn't aware of his project and I was involved in quite a few other things, so I was a bit wary of committing time to anything else.

We met over a cup of coffee and talked about Edel initially, and he asked me about how I felt about the 'situation'. He was tentative about discussing his idea at first, although he was open about how he felt regarding the homosexuality of his children. He talked about his concern for them and their future, his worries regarding their lives being lonely, ridiculed, maybe victimised. He asked me how I felt about Kevin's sexuality.

I told him that I had known for a long time that Kevin was gay. I was always accepting of his sexuality. I felt, and still feel, that our sexuality is part of the creative process. In other words, it is God's plan, and we have no business making judgments about whether there is a right or wrong way to express our sexuality, providing we are not exploiting another person, and that applies to all relationships.

He said that he hadn't thought of it like that, and confided that Anne and he had cried when they had talked about it. I admitted that I had occasions when I was enraged when Kevin was bullied and victimised by some of his peers, and if I let myself think about the behaviour of homophobic people I sometimes felt, and still feel, afraid for Kevin.

Peter talked about his project. He talked about forming a **SUPPORT** group for parents whose children were gay. We tossed around a few ideas and I explained that I was already involved in too many committees, but that I would attend and join the group in any other way.

When Kevin was little he was gentle and sensitive and a huge worrier. When he started to play with neighbours' children while still in junior primary school, he was called gay by the other children. His teacher once asked me to come in to discuss him. Her worry was that he played alone. He never got involved with the rough and tumble of the school play. I asked him when we got home why he played alone - he replied that the other boys were too rough. After that I became particularly aware that he was different, serious and sensitive, and I tried to take account of this when dealing with him.

The teenaged years are a difficult time. Add to this the difficulty of not feeling accepted by one's straight peers, at a time when you're discovering your sexuality, must have been particularly difficult. I'm glad that Kevin, Edel and the other friends in their group had each other for support.

I have spoken to mothers of gay children who were disappointed about the future prospect of their children. Maybe victimisation at work, attack by homophobic others, the loss of potential grandchildren, the fear of AIDS, parents' fear of ridicule from their friends and neighbours, the fear that there was something wrong with them. Such a lot of fear.

Fear is an absence of awareness that love is what we are. Once we give attention to our fears, they grow and awareness of love diminishes. I was very lucky that I didn't let those fears overpower me. I am still concerned about homophobic behaviour and how it affects society and gays in particular, but I think that says more about homophobes than me.

When I tell my peers that Kevin is gay, often there is

often an embarrassed silence. I feel that sometimes the embarrassment is for me, other times it's because they feel there is something wrong. I always try to disarm their embarrassment by explaining that I don't have a problem with it.

Fifteen years later Kevin is now an adult and Peter and Edel are no longer here. While things have moved on in many ways for both us as a family and as a society, my friends' embarrassment shows that there is still very much a need for the support that Peter was trying to put in place. What Peter wanted to achieve was a safe place where parents and family could be completely honest and open about how they felt about the issue at hand.

Sexuality, relationships, and growing up are human challenges facing everyone, gay or straight. Peter seemed to appreciate that these human challenges are much more manageable with the compassion and support of others.

LIBERATE

by Suzanne Stafford

I walked into the room, and there she was, bold as brass, cheeky wee face, sat with her friend whom I already knew.

Without any control whatsoever, a huge smile stretched across my face, and before I knew it I was marching across the room to introduce myself. I took her hand in mine and held it for what seemed like a long time staring into her beautiful brown eyes.

Who is she? Where has she come from? And most importantly why have I NEVER met her before now?

Mmmmm ... Edel, what a sweet name that matched such a sweet little face. My only thought was to keep her attention on me (selfish, I know), but the last thing I wanted right now were cute young lesbians walking through the door. This was in our local LGBT drop-in centre and there was plenty of competition as it was.

Conversation happened easily and flowed so naturally between us. I felt I had already known her for a long time; she had that effect on people, she made them comfortable and made friends easily. I tried to learn everything I could about her in the shortest time possible, asking questions about where she worked, where she grew up, what car she drove, etc.

The thing that devastated me most was the discovery that she lived in Cork and was only home for a few days. I was already picturing the commute!

As our unfortunately short meeting came to a close, I really wanted to kiss her, but I couldn't. I was awkward, I was shy and I could sense that she felt the same. However, she did mention that she was in town until Monday, and that was my chance.

I was celebrating my 22nd birthday that coming Saturday, and as it was my first birthday since my 'coming out', it was to be a women's-only party.

It would be great to invite her along, so I did. She accepted, promising me she would be there, and I told her to bring her friends too. Before we parted ways I insisted she repeat my address over and over so she would never forget.

That was April 1999, I remember it like it was yesterday.

I woke up on the day of my 22nd birthday so excited; I had so many wonderful friends all coming together in one place. Such diversity - my straight friends, my lesbian friends and my undecided friends. All from such different walks of life, all women, all beautiful.

My four-year-old son was off to stay with his granny and granddad for the weekend. I felt so free, so **LIBERATED** and alive, and extremely hopeful that maybe my new friend would show up. I tried my best not to let my hopes build up, but it was impossible. My heart skipped a beat with every knock on the door.

I had been out for less than a year and I had met a lot of women and made some fabulous new friends. Though I had a few short-term relationships, I really didn't see myself finding or meeting someone that I could see as a more long-term thing.

Besides, my future wasn't the type I reckoned many of these women would want to share. I was a single mum from a local authority housing estate. It wasn't going to be easy, and it would have to be a very brave woman to take on me and all my baggage.

Nonetheless, I was happy with my lot. My son was my life, and everything else was secondary. It may not have always looked that way to some, but no one can dispute that parenting alone can be a very daunting and lonely place, even with the support of family. Especially when you feel like you should be doing all the same things that your peers are doing at that age.

What my peers were doing wasn't exactly what I wanted to be doing, though. I surrounded myself with people I believed to be security, people who would keep me safe in a world that petrified me. I needed to fit in to survive.

I had done what I thought to be the normal thing - I got myself a boyfriend, stayed with him for a few years and then had a baby. That seemed to be the way to do things.

I had a friend, when I was 15 or 16, who came out as

a lesbian. Her girlfriend was a little older and much more butch. I admired them and loved to hang out with them, but I never gave a second thought to thinking that maybe I, too, could be gay.

Sure, I had a boyfriend! And he was the best boyfriend, especially since he had taken himself off to Mountjoy Prison for a few years, leaving me, at the age of 18, and my infant alone in our council house.

This turned out to be the greatest gift ever given to me, because it changed my life forever. I went about discovering myself for the first time, and with the help of some good friends and some great youth workers, I slowly learned to like and accept myself in a whole new way. I began to read, paint and dance, I felt creative. All my senses woke up, I began to believe in myself and felt that anything was possible.

My new way of thinking brought with it a new wave of friends. These new friends were colourful and interesting. I was studying and had gotten on to a community employment scheme, which, after a year or two, led to gainful employment. I found myself involved in a cross-border young mothers' project, and at this time I began to realise that I had sexual feelings towards my own gender.

One of the project leaders made an impression on me from the moment I met her. I guessed she was gay and was intrigued and found myself going home in the evenings thinking about her. I can't say that this was a huge revelation for me or that I was shocked, I just thought it was something in which I might indulge at some stage in my life.

I was happy to keep this new information to myself, but began to suss out where I might find other young gay people in this small town. That didn't take long, and shortly they seemed to be everywhere now that my eyes were a little more open.

I felt the first sting when my work with this woman had finished, as I never spoke to her about my feelings and I would probably never see her again. It was time for me to explore these new feelings somewhere safe, somewhere local.

I started to attend the local LGBT centre and its monthly discos. It was at this time I met my first girlfriend and was 'outed' by some of my straight friends who I had trusted. That's when it became a problem; my son would be ridiculed, I would get shouted at on the street, and I became so familiar with the derogatory terms associated with homosexuality, and comments referring to the abuse of my child and being a 'double adapter' (that one stuck because I used to have a boyfriend).

I wasn't really sure whether I was gay or bi, but I was with women only for 10 years, so I guess that made me a lesbian for that period. I think I always knew deep down that I was bisexual, and I did often think one day I would like more children. I felt less accepted by the gay community if I admitted my bisexuality, so it was something I kept mostly to myself and close friends.

Back to the night of my 22nd party. I had dressed my best and nervously answered the door to each visitor. There was plenty there, and it was a great night. I was very drunk by 11pm, but regardless continued into the small hours.

Edel never showed up. I woke up on a couch, cold, hungover and surrounded by other bodies. I reflected on the night as I tidied up and wondered when, if ever, would I see her again.

Weeks passed, and my normal routine continued. I really longed to meet someone just like her; someone I truly believed would understand me and have the same interests.

Out of the blue one day a letter came to my house addressed to a Suzanne Bentley. My surname was not Bentley, but the female-on-female symbol on the back of the envelope made me pretty sure it was for me.

I opened it and looked straight to the end to see by whom it was signed. It was from Edel. I was so delighted. She apologised profusely for not coming to my party and blamed her friends for taking her out of town and refusing to come back with her. She ended the letter by saying she was hoping to see me at the annual Cork women's weekend.

I had no intentions of going to that, but now I really, really wanted to. That wasn't going to be possible – it was difficult to get care for my son for the whole weekend, with my father being sick, and financially I wasn't in a position to go. I sadly asked my friends who were going to send my love if they met her there. To this day I am glad I didn't go because it turned out she wasn't there either - she had gone home that same weekend.

A short while later, after yet another drunken night out in Dublin, I nursed my very bad hangover in the centre, moaning about the embarrassing antics of the previous night. One of my friends informed me that I had had a visitor, but she wouldn't tell me who it was.

As I was about to leave, the doorbell sounded, and in fell Edel and her friend, fairly intoxicated. Edel arrived with her mountain bike in tow, ripped jeans, happy smile and unapologetic laughter. At first I thought the friend must be her girlfriend, but her behaviour towards me soon ruled that out, as her flirting was so obvious in her little drunken stupor. I was silently thrilled and extremely entertained.

That night became the first night of the best six years of my life.

It all moved very quickly after that. Edel moved in within weeks. We had become the town's golden couple, everyone loved to see us coming. We were madly in love. Her friends became my friends and mine hers. I loved everything about her little tomboy look, her quirky ways, her humour. We spent a lot of our time laughing.

It wasn't quite as easy a start for her and my son. She had never spent much time with small children, and at the age of four he felt like he wasn't getting all of mammy's attention with this new woman around. I am sure it must have been very confusing for him to see his mammy kissing a girl, but we agreed we wouldn't hide our affection for each other from him, and we never did.

Edel was very careful not to win his love over by spoiling him or trying to buy it, so it was a beautiful, slow process of him learning to trust her and becoming familiar with her. Before too long I was almost jealous of their relationship, as he found it easier to talk to her than me at times. I had to be the mammy and daddy, so I couldn't be all fun – I had to be the disciplinarian, too.

My parents weren't at all shocked or fazed by my coming out. They were quite liberal and reckoned there is 'one' in every family, I just happened to be the one in ours. My parents and siblings adored Edel, I used to say butter wouldn't melt because she could do no wrong in their eyes.

I know it wasn't quite so easy for Edel. I believe her coming out was a bit more difficult for her parents to understand, and because she was so young when she discovered her sexuality, I am guessing they hoped it was a phase. I think she had some dark times in her teens; it must be hard trying to accept yourself when the people who love you most are struggling to accept you.

I am sure it didn't help when she moved in with a lone parent from an estate with an awful reputation. In fairness they were right to be worried about that, as we often got shouted at, our windows were broken, and the car vandalised. The worst was Edel's first little scooter (her Vespa, her pride and joy) was taken and burned out around the corner - all because we were gay.

Protecting my son while trying to teach him acceptance was somewhat difficult. But we stuck it out and stuck together nonetheless.

About a year into our relationship I got my dream job in youth work, and less than a year later so did Edel. Working for different companies, doing the same type of work, was great as we could discuss it and help each other at the end of the day. It also meant we were in a position to move into rented accommodation. We spent a few years at this address where the three of us were very contented and happy.

My son made great friends and we had the privilege of having almost everything we wanted. We had two or three holidays a year, socialised as much as we wanted, and both had new cars. We were grateful and happy. We were just like any other couple, but with our new financial independence came its own problems.

We both had darkness in our pasts, and I found light at the bottom of a bottle. We both did, but it became my crutch, and I used it! That brought with it some of our problems, and since Edel wasn't great with confrontation, I was happy to ignore my own behaviour.

Hindsight is a great thing, and I couldn't see my flaws. Looking back now, I can see where I went wrong.

We carried on regardless and began to make plans to buy a house, which personally made me scared stupid. It was a commitment that really frightened me, but Edel knew it was the right thing to do - though I didn't and at times felt a little bit pushed into it. It was going to be our dream comes true. And the day we moved into our own house felt like the best day of our lives.

Unfortunately, it was short-lived. Sometimes life throws things at you that you can't control, for which you can never prepare yourself, and what life threw at us at the age of 27, I really wasn't fit to deal with. It pains me to think about it even now.

Shortly after our six-year anniversary Edel came home, from a night out with a friend, looking tired and distraught. My naivety is something else! I really didn't see it coming. She told me she was leaving, and she meant it.

My life felt like it had just crumbled all around me. I didn't sleep in our bed any more as I couldn't bear it. I slept on the couch or the floor, depending on how drunk I got. I was unwilling to accept that my drinking and staying out was that bad, as that was what we had done for years. Now I was doing it alone, as much as she was coping on her own. I had my blinkers on. It didn't help that she believed I was cheating, though now I couldn't blame her.

Thankfully I had the pleasure of her beautiful company for a night some time after we broke up, giving me the chance to explain, to talk when she was ready to listen. She did, and for that I am grateful.

I was one of the luckiest women on this planet to have shared such a magical and wonderful experience with one of life's true gems. She brought light and laughter into mine and my son's life.

If I knew then what I know now ... They say that time is a healer ... it's all we can hope for.

THANK

by Collette O'Regan

Peter made an appointment with us to come and see the drop-in centre Dundalk Outcomers. It was still in the basement of the Georgian building at that time. But of course it looked wonderful because it was all nicely painted - bright and cheerful - to buck the expectation that basements are dreary and not happy places to build foundations for transforming lives.

I remember Bernie and I showed him around, we made tea and we drank it together sitting on the couch. He asked us about our own story of how we told our parents that we were gay. Bernie said, "Sure, I didn't need to tell me mam, 'cos the whole town knows who I am", or something like that. And I told him that I hadn't told my parents yet. I told him that I was weighing up how much I needed them to know versus how much they needed to know – their need versus my-need approach. And I told him I felt their need not to know was more important for now.

And I remember how he said that this approach was not fair to me, and that it also wasn't fair on them because maybe they wanted to support me, maybe they wanted to know the full story, etc. He said I was being robbed of my parents' love and support for this part of my life, and I was equally robbing my parents of their chance to show me this kind of love.

I remember thinking, "What a wonderful father this man is ... how lucky Edel and Martin are to have such a loving, supportive, brave father". I also realised that I had never thought of my dilemma from the perspective he shared.

And so he gave me pause for thought. He helped me realise for the first time, in a very real way - because he was so real - that it was not selfish of me to want my parents to know that I'm gay. He helped me realise that it is normal for a daughter or son to want this from their parents. It is normal to wish to be known and accepted for who you are, wholly and truly. Such is the experience of being loved. Peter helped me realise it is OK to expect this from my parents.

Later, I did tell my parents. And in their own time, they did respond wonderfully, full of support and full of love. And I remember feeling lucky to have finally found this response from them. I remember a feeling of completion, of peace, of truth and arrival. And I remember my encounter with Peter with deep gratitude and as a gift to me.

Meeting Peter, brief though it was, turned out to be a significant step on my journey towards coming out to my parents. I have never underestimated the potential of brief encounters since.

May Peter be resting in peace and surrounded by love wherever he dwells. May these memories of his wonderful love for his rainbow kids inspire others like me to dare to believe in the immense love parents have for their children, and the potential of that love to embrace all of who we are.

And may Peter inspire more of us to take a step towards trusting our parents, and equally inspire our parents to take a step towards accepting us.

THANK you, Peter.

We invite you to write your story for inclusion on our website or future editions of this book and email to info@myson-mydaughter-myself.org or upload via our website www.myson-mydaughter-myself.org.

Made in the USA
Middletown, DE
21 February 2021

33965468R00078